KILLING MY OLD MAN

Being the Person God Sees in Me

Rodney Peavy

ISBN 979-8-88644-477-3 (Paperback)
ISBN 979-8-88644-478-0 (Digital)

Unless otherwise noted all Bible quotes are from the Holy Bible: King James Version. Carol Stream, IL: Barbour Publishing, Inc., 2003. Other translations quoted include:

The Christian Standard Bible. Copyright © 2017 by Holman Bible Publishers. Used by permission. Christian Standard Bible®, and CSB® are federally registered trademarks of Holman Bible Publishers, all rights reserved.

"Scripture quotations are from the ESV® Bible (The Holy Bible, English Standard Version®), copyright © 2001 by Crossway, a publishing ministry of Good News Publishers. Used by permission. All rights reserved. The ESV text may not be quoted in any publication made available to the public by a Creative Commons license. The ESV may not be translated into any other language."

Scripture quotations marked HCSB are taken from the Holman Christian Standard Bible®, Copyright © 1999, 2000, 2002, 2003, 2009 by Holman Bible Publishers. Used by permission. Holman Christian Standard Bible®, Holman CSB®, and HCSB® are federally registered trademarks of Holman Bible Publishers.

"Scripture quotations taken from the (NASB®) New American Standard Bible®, Copyright © 1960, 1971, 1977, 1995, 2020 by The Lockman Foundation. Used by permission. All rights reserved. www.lockman.org"

THE HOLY BIBLE, NEW INTERNATIONAL VERSION®, NIV® Copyright © 1973, 1978, 1984, 2011 by Biblica, Inc.™ Used by permission. All rights reserved worldwide.

Covenant Books
11661 Hwy 707
Murrells Inlet, SC 29576
www.covenantbooks.com

For my crazy family…
Without whom I'd be lost.

Searcher of Hearts, it is a good day to me when
thou givest me a glimpse of myself.

—A Puritan prayer taken from
The Valley of Vision

CONTENTS

PREFACE

I must admit, this endeavor is much more than just another writing project or assignment for me. It is far more personal. It began as an exploration of Romans 6–8. I was attempting to fully grasp why it is that these three chapters are often looked upon as being the pinnacle of the book of the Bible often referred to as the "Gospel of Grace." It was an honest attempt on my part to move from a head knowledge of these truths to a heart knowledge. Unexpectedly, this exploration evolved into something so intimate in nature that my first thought was to keep it locked away in a place where only I could see it and then turn to it only to firm up my own heart when needed. Nevertheless, as God often seems to do with such thoughts, I have received an overwhelming sense that the truth shown to me in the writing of these pages is not a truth to keep to myself, but a truth that might serve to encourage all who find themselves in need of being reminded of their identity as God sees it and the freedom that accompanies such a discovery.

This book has been long in coming and not an easy accomplishment to say the least. Little did I know that my digestion of these three chapters of Romans would be accompanied by a period of soul searching, self-loathing, and personal crisis in my spiritual and private life. To many onlookers, the inner struggles of this period of my life probably went unnoticed. However, to me it was a time of deep questioning and emotional striving, the likes of which I had, to this point in life, never endured. It was a time of ups and downs, of ping-ponging between depression and expression. It was at times miserable and at times joyous. Suffice it to say, it was a time that I pray I never have to relive and a time for which I would not trade for anything. It was a time of molding and shaping, and I consider it a personal treasure. It was no coincidence that God led me to this longing when he did. It was through this period in my life that God revealed himself to me in a new and dynamic way. He showed me the pain of grace and the healing of surrender. He has reminded me of who I am to him and, most importantly, who he is to me. It has been truly liberating.

My prayer is that all who come to this book searching for answers and personal change will find themselves in an ever-growing closer relationship with the Giver of All Answers. Prepare to see yourself differently. Prepare to meet the stranger in the mirror, perhaps for the first time. Prepare to hate what you see and to love what you see. Prepare to be challenged and possibly even a little frustrated along the way, but nonetheless better for it. Most importantly, prepare to encounter the God who loves that person in the mirror more than you ever thought possible. Prepare your heart to finally put aside that old man you thought you were and become the person God sees in you, loved and lovely.

Rodney Peavy

1

The Man in the Mirror

I have never met a man who has given
me as much trouble as myself.
—Dwight L. Moody

Knowing this, that our old man is crucified with *him*, that the body
of sin might be destroyed, that henceforth we should not serve sin.
—Romans 6:6 (KJV)

What a loser!

That was my thought as I stood in front of the mirror staring into my own disenchanted face. I am a loser. A hypocrite. A complete and perpetual disappointment. At best, I am a jerk. I can't give you a date when this mirrored revelation occurred. I can't because it has happened more than once and, admittedly, not all at once. In fact, it happens quite often, usually following a spiritual failure of some sort. I say I'll never do it again. I vow to do better. I make promises to God and myself to never repeat the same stupid mistake. I even expend great amounts of energy to avoid the private slip ups that have so convicted my heart. Then it happens.

Bam!

I find myself once more standing in front of the mirror asking "Again?" What a loser…

You may be questioning your decision to read this book as you read this confession. Who is this person, this *loser* that I am reading? Well, he is a person in good company. Let's be honest. Haven't we all found ourselves in front of that mirror and asking, "Again?"? Haven't we all found ourselves repeating the same old mistakes after making a genuine vow to never return to them? Haven't we all been rocked by the revelation that despite all our best intentions, we are still prone to sin? Some sins more than others. If my old man is crucified, why do I keep running into him so often?

If we are not careful, it can become a lifelong cycle of self-contempt. Sin. Conviction. Repentance. Promise to do better. Repeat. Sin. Conviction. Repentance. Promise. Repeat. If it happens often enough, the broken promises and pledges we make to God can become such a source of shame and self-hatred that we no longer find ourselves convicted or repenting. We give up on ourselves, and ultimately, we give up on God. Our hearts become hardened, and we find ourselves stuck in this cycle of making the "same old mistakes." Could it be perhaps due to a misunderstanding of our own nature and our role in overcoming the sins which so heavily beset us? Or am I truly beyond the grace of God?

What is the "same old mistake" to which I am personally referring? Well, sorry, but that is for me to know and for you to never find out. It is my business. I have mine. You have yours. I won't ask you if you promise that you won't ask me. We all have our personal demons with which we struggle. It wasn't until recently that I fully appreciated the significance of this struggle within myself. It was in one of these man-in-the-mirror moments that I realized just how ugly the "old man" within me really could be.

While I've never considered myself to be perfect, I have thought of myself as a fairly good person. After all, I don't curse. I don't use drugs or drink alcohol. I am a faithful husband, father, and friend. I even go out of my way to not hurt others. In fact, I have even gone so far as to dedicate my life to serving God and helping others through vocational ministry. I am a pastor.

(Okay, now imagine me somewhat conceitedly patting myself on the back... Thanks.)

So if all this is true, if I am such a good person, why can't I stop doing certain things I don't want to do? Why can't I stop having such un-Christian thoughts? Why do I still struggle with pride? Why do I still struggle with selfishness? Why can't I stop repeating the "same old mistakes"? What kind of person am I really?

Well, despite all the good of which I may be capable, if I am going to be honest, I must admit that at my very best, I am equally capable of some of the cruelest, most despicable behavior one can imagine. Even if only in my mind and heart, I have still cheated, lied, blasphemed, stolen, committed adultery, and even murdered. I am selfish, prideful, dirty-minded, arrogant, and devious. Of this and much more, I am guilty. Guilty as sin.

What? Who is this? Who am I reading? A murderer? A cheat? An adulterer? A liar? Well…yes! In the hidden caverns of my heart, I have murdered those who oppose me. In the unseen parts of my inner man, I have cheated those whom I love. Though my outward man appears to stand tall and mostly unblemished to the outside world, inside I stumble and fall daily. In there, where others can't see, I find myself doing and thinking things that do more than just make me blush—they make me sick. Yet there it is. That is the ugly truth of my hidden existence.

It has taken me decades to fully grasp the reality of my inner struggle. Growing up in a society that promotes the relative virtue of mankind and his endeavors; the depravity of mankind, specifically my own depravity, has taken some time to truly understand and appreciate. The irony of this middle-aged epiphany is that the accepting of my own fallacy has not led to a life of discouragement and hopelessness as one might expect. In fact, it has had just the opposite effect. Coming to terms with my weaknesses has actually broken me free from the cycle of self-hatred that led me to my original loser in the mirror moment. It is a freedom that every child of God is meant to carry. It is the paradox of grace.

Here is a life-changing truth. Take it and hold on to it. Get a life-altering super determined spiritual vice grip hold on this truth. Here it is. God's love for me has absolutely nothing to do with my performance!

So if you are feeling like a loser yourself in regard to your spiritual condition, hidden or otherwise, then I have some good news for you. Like I've already said, you are in good company. This time, I am not talking about myself. I am referring to a different loser. In fact, this person didn't refer to himself as a loser. He called himself a wretch! More specifically, a wretched man.

A wretch or wretched. It's all the same. The word itself in the modern English paints a pretty vivid picture of how this otherwise spiritual giant viewed himself. It is an image of revulsion, personal disgust, and misery. Yet to most, this person would probably be considered the spiritual superior to almost everyone that is living or has ever lived, short of Jesus himself. I, of course, am referring to the Apostle Paul, pastor to the early church, author of the majority of the New Testament, author of "the great love chapter" of 1 Corinthians 13 and author of Romans, often called the gospel of grace. He is considered the first missionary to the gentiles, a man who stood before kings proclaiming the gospel, a man who would endure beatings, shipwrecks, and snakebites with joy as an inevitable part of his "high calling" and a man that would ultimately give his life for the sake of his faith. And oh yeah, a man that was to himself a wretch…

What would cause such a man to refer to himself as a wretched man?

While we do not know specifics of the occasion, we do have the benefit of his shared insight. Paul had his own man-in-the-mirror moment. It is recorded for us in Romans 7. While the whole chapter addresses his inner condition, his personal angst really surfaces in verse 15 and reaches a climax in verse 24.

> For I do not understand what I am doing,
> because I do not practice what I want to do, but
> I do what I hate.
> And if I do what I do not want to do, I agree
> with the law that it is good.
> So now I am no longer the one doing it, but
> it is sin living in me.

> For I know that nothing good lives in me,
> that is, in my flesh. For the desire to do what is
> good is with me, but there is no ability to do it.
>
> For I do not do the good that I want to do,
> but I practice the evil that I do not want to do.
>
> Now if I do what I do not want, I am no
> longer the one doing it, but it is the sin that lives
> in me.
>
> So I discover this principle: When I want to
> do what is good, evil is with me.
>
> For in my inner self I joyfully agree with
> God's law.
>
> But I see a different law in the parts of my
> body, waging war against the law of my mind and
> taking me prisoner to the law of sin in the parts
> of my body.
>
> What a wretched man I am! Who will res-
> cue me from this dying body? (Rom. 7:15–24
> HCSB)

In this passage, we have one of the purest expressions of personal frustration recorded in all of scripture. It is also one of the most relatable.

After expounding on the role and effect of the law and sin in the human heart in the verses leading up to this, Paul then goes into this tongue twisting rant of self-expression in verse 15. A God-inspired tongue-twisting rant, but a rant, nonetheless. He basically questions why it is that he keeps finding himself doing things he doesn't want to do and not doing the things he wants. It ends with his crying out, "What a wretched man I am!" This was his "not again" frustrated man-in-the-mirror moment. Why can't I stop doing these things and be the man I want to be and that God wants me to be?

We are not certain as to what sin specifically Paul was referring to when he spoke of "the evil I do not want to do" (vs. 19). That is okay. In fact, I believe it is intentional. If we knew specifically, then we might conclude that the principles found in this passage do not apply to my specific struggle. Thankfully, God in his wisdom left the specifics out so that we can see ourselves in the words. It is Paul's struggle. It is my struggle. It is everyone's struggle. This is one of the most personal passages in all of scripture. Read it in that context.

However, for candor's sake, it should probably be mentioned how through the centuries; it has been fervently debated as to whether or not Paul is referring to believers or nonbelievers in this passage, to himself before or after his Road to Damascus conversion. Some even go so far as to try to assign the principles found here to different stages in the life of a believer or nonbeliever. While there are convincing arguments on either side of the debate, I tend to lean toward the thought that Paul was speaking about believers. I feel he was speaking of himself and all believers in general after a point of conversion as they are maturing in their faith. His use of the present tense throughout the passage as well as its relation to chapter 8 would suggest that he is talking about himself in his here and now and the Christian experience in general. Chapter 8 of the book of Romans seems to deal mostly with the process of sanctification and the role of the Holy Spirit in the life of a maturing believer. If you ascribe to this interpretation as I do, then you see the inner struggle as occurring in the heart of a man that was by all accounts a follower of Jesus Christ. A dedicated follower of Jesus Christ. In fact, I think it safe to say an extremely over the top dedicated follower of Jesus Christ. Yet through it all, he still had to fight his old nature.

Most importantly for me, more personally than intellectually, I lean toward this interpretation because I have seen it at work many times within my own heart and in the lives of others. Christians aren't perfect. We sometimes make mistakes. Trust me. I've made some whoppers. We also sometimes repeat those mistakes. There are times when I don't "feel" saved. This is a simple reality. It doesn't change what Jesus has done for me or my love for him. It is just the simple truth of the battle that we are fighting.

As I pastor, I have sat across the desk from many a frustrated disciple that felt as Paul seemed to feel in Romans 7. Pastor, if I am a new creation, then why can't I stop? Why can't I give up this addiction? Why can't I conquer this temptation to which I keep giving in?

If I am a new creation, why I am still struggling with the old temptations? Why do I keep going to the bottle? Why do I keep returning to this toxic relationship? Why do I keep telling lies when I know to tell the truth? Why do I still gossip? Why can't I stop having these lustful thoughts? Why I can't I beat this porn addiction? I love Jesus. I really do… So why can't I just quit once and for all? I've heard it countless times. It's real life.

We will repeatedly address Romans 7 and all of this in greater detail in the following chapters. For now, I just want to encourage you with this simple revelation. Put aside the debate as to when Paul wrote this passage and put aside the question as to the meaning of his "evil practice" (vs. 15) that led him to this crying out. Put all that aside and you are left with a man that loved God and his law deeply, but still didn't always do what God wanted. Here was a man that longed to live a life of holiness and yet often fell short of his own expectations. And it made him feel like a wretch.

And let's not forget that it is Paul. This is the great Apostle Paul we are talking about for goodness' sake! This is Paul saying that evil is always right there with him (vs. 21). Now, if he had these feelings, isn't it only expected that I might as well? After all, I am no Paul. If it is true of Paul, is it not also true of me?

While it may not seem appropriate to find comfort in the struggle of another in their spiritual lives, I must admit that there is a part of me that finds great solace in the very real and down-to-earth admission expressed in this chapter of Romans by the great Apostle. Put simply, I find that I am not alone in feeling the way I do. You are not alone in feeling the way you do either. As mature as Paul was in his faith, he still looked at himself in the mirror and saw a wretched man. If Paul could feel that way, then just maybe I am not the loser I once thought.

When you stand in front of your mirror filled with self-doubt, you are not alone either. You are standing beside Paul, myself, and countless others. You are standing next to all the other wretches! And you're in good company. So don't think your situation is hopeless. Don't think for a moment that no one else knows what you are feeling! Don't think you are somehow beyond redemption or at the very least beyond relief! You are not.

In fact, our Lord specializes in taking the losers of the world and using them in ways we would never expect. The Bible is filled with such wretched men and women. Everything from prostitutes, murderers, and even to what would be called terrorists in today's vernacular have been changed by God and used to carry out God's will in his word and world. So don't think that somehow you went too far this time, and that God has somehow finally had enough. God is too big and his love too great to ever run out of patience with his children. Likewise, it is God's area of expertise to use what we might think is unusable and to mend what we think is beyond repair. It is what he does best.

However, to break the cycle of self-contempt, we must first come to terms with the struggle within ourselves. We are often quick to recognize the struggles between good and evil out in the world or in others. But what about the struggle right here within ourselves? Remember, Paul said evil was always right there with him when he wanted to do good (vs. 21). He finds it a law working within himself. What about us? We cannot ignore it. Paul often calls it the flesh. Call it our sin nature or our fallen nature. Call it human nature. Call it our bent. Call it the way I was born. Call it what you will, but count on this. You *will* wrestle with it eventually if you wish to grow and mature in your faith.

If you want to find yourself in front of that mirror of regret less often, if you want to put away that old man or at least encounter him less often, which I am assuming is why you are reading this book, then you must learn to not fear that face that lingers in those background shadows. You know the one I am talking about, the face that only you see. He's that doppelganger that lives in the dark caverns and crevices of your mind, always there, warring against your desire to do good. It's the you that you hope no one else ever sees in you. Yes, he can be ugly. He can even be "wretched." Nonetheless, he is part of us and we must endeavor to ever fight him.

He is the old man. And he can be put away with God's help. He can be killed.

Looking Even Deeper

Personal/Group Discussion and Application

1. Read Romans 6:1–11.

2. In Romans 6:6, we are told that our old man has been crucified and that we are no longer slaves to sin. What do you think this means?

3. Can you personally relate to the author's "man-in-the-mirror moment"? How so?

4. We often call them besetting sins. How do these repetitious sins or broken vows make you feel and how do they you think they affect your relationship with God?

5. Do you agree with the author's statement: "God's love for me has absolutely nothing to do with my performance"? How does your opinion on this statement affect your spiritual growth?

6. In Romans 7:14–25, Paul decries his own personal struggle with sin. What is your theory on this outcry? How does it make you feel knowing Paul struggled in this manner?

7. Pray that God will help you to be honest with yourself and most importantly with him concerning your old man nature and for his help to overcome it.

2

KISSING FROGS

Never trust a dog to watch your food.
>—Saint Patrick

I have a word for you. I know your whole life story. I know
every skeleton in your closet. I know every moment of sin,
shame, dishonesty and degraded love that has darkened your
past. Right now I know your shallow faith, your feeble prayer
life, your inconsistent discipleship. And my word is this: I
dare you to trust that I love you just as you are, and not as you
should be. Because you're never going to be as you should be.
>—Brennan Manning

Indeed, there is not a righteous man on earth who
continually does good and never sins.
>—Ecclesiastes 7:20

I have four adopted children, three sons and one daughter. Each one
was only a couple of years younger than the prior. Each came to be
family at the early age of three or less. It is safe to say that there was
never a dull moment around our house, especially when they were
younger. I would like to say that it got calmer as they grew older, but
I cannot. I am dedicated to intellectual honesty in this book after all.

Once upon a time, in a backyard not unlike your own, my oldest two sons convinced their younger sister that if she would simply kiss a toad frog they had caught, that he would surely turn into Prince Charming, just like they do in the fairy tales and Disney movies. So trusting in her older siblings, she puckered up and planted one on that frog. Needless to say, her misplaced trust in her brothers did not lead to a fairy tale ending. He did not magically transform into a handsome prince. The only transformation that took place was playtime changing to a time out for the boys. However, it does make for good family laughs and memories today.

Yet as silly as that is, I wonder how many of us toads today wish it were as simple as a kiss to change us to something more attractive?

I think many of us approach our faith in that mindset. It's as if we think coming to Christ is like receiving that kiss, from the frog's perspective, of course. We think as soon as we commit to living for Christ that somehow all our warts and bumps magically go away and we become suddenly handsome and attractive. When Jesus kisses us with his salvation, we are suddenly changed into sinless perfect people. Sadly, it does not take very long for the new believer to discover that it doesn't work that way. In fact, I have always thought that we do a disservice to new converts by not warning them ahead of time that they are still prone to sin. Nothing can dampen the spirits of a new believer more quickly than finding out that you are still a sinner after all. Too often, we go into it thinking that now, once and for all, I will not have to deal with all the guilt and shame anymore. No more stumbling. No more slipping up. No more falling short. Then guess what happens: One day, you open your mouth to speak and…

Crrrooooakkk!

We look in the mirror expecting to see princes and princesses, and all we see is warts and bumps. We expect to see prince charming and all we find is a toad. Instead of seeing the new creation, we see the old us that we would like to forget.

Why are we so surprised by our sinful tendencies?

Now that three of these four kids are either married or moved out and the other one is older, I find I spend less time refereeing between the kids, and I have more free time to do things I enjoy.

Selfish? Maybe. But true. One thing I have found especially true, though, is that my enjoyments have changed since they were young enough to try kissing frogs.

For example, the older I get, the more I enjoy reading. It is not just that it requires less physical stress for my aging body. I genuinely enjoy the mental challenge of reading a good book. I try to stay away from fluff reading and intentionally look for books that are going to produce growth in me.

More than that, though, the older I get, the older the books I read seem to be getting. I am not sure why that is the case exactly. I will not pretend to understand the psychology of it. Nonetheless, it is true. I am sure there is a reason. (By the way, the irony of a new author extoling the values of older literary works is not wasted on me.) Perhaps it is because I find the older works more life-changing and challenging. It is also perhaps due to the fact that they have withstood the changing trials and tests of time and culture. If they can do that, then they are worth a read.

I find myself more often than not going back to some of the old Christian classics. There is an endless supply of classics from which to discover new favorites. I enjoy reading the writings of the early church fathers. I enjoy reading things from the Middle Ages. I especially enjoy reading devotionals and prayers from the Puritan period of history. From priests, monks, Puritan preachers and even writers as close back as a century ago, there seems to be a common quality found in their antiquated writings. They were brutally honest. They knew they were toads and they didn't try to hide it.

It is not that writers of today are not honest. There are many great ones out there that are much better at it than I am or will ever be. There are some that definitely have a greater intellect than me. Many of them are committed to teaching biblical truth and are dedicated to that end. But the writings of these long-gone Christians seem to reveal a keener understanding of their own sin nature and more importantly, their need for help beyond their own abilities, than do contemporary writers and teachers. So much of today's writing is about how we can pull ourselves up by our bootstraps with hard work and determination and can by sheer willpower overcome any obstacle. They praise human ingenuity and ability. We are given well-meaning formulas to apply and outlines to follow as guides to achieving spiritual success. As if it were that simple…

These older works, however, are written by people that seemed to have a different approach. They were quick to acknowledge their inability to defeat their old man. They have since completed their race and have finally killed their old nature with which we still struggle with daily. Did their approach work? Hopefully. Yet while they were still living and writing, they wrestled just as you and I do today. And they did not mince words when it comes to describing it.

One of my favorite books is called *The Valley of Vision*. It is a collection of Puritan prayers and poems. It is a collection of quite possibly some of the most beautiful writings of the period. I have a leather-bound version that I keep with me at all times. I read it as a devotional addendum to my daily Bible devotions. I recommend you do it as well. It is obviously man's thoughts and not inspired on the level of scripture. It is, nonetheless, inspirational. There are many reasons why I love it, but probably the most obvious is the candor in which those Puritans prayed.

One example is found in the prayer titled "Mortification." The praying believer mourns his "sins," "deficiencies," and "backslidings." He then says this,

> I have light enough to see my darkness,
> sensibility enough to feel the hardness of my
>   heart,
> spirituality enough to mourn my want of a heav-
>   enly mind;
> but I might have had more,
> I ought to have had more.

The writer and praying Christian believes that even his tacit understanding of his corrupted nature is not experienced near deeply enough in relation to his actual sinfulness. In other words, as bad as it seems, reality is probably much, much worse. In another prayer titled "Purification," the writer asks for God's help to remain aware of his sin. He says, "I sin-Grant that I may never cease grieving because of it."

Really? Who prays like that?

Who asks God to help me not forget just how rotten I am?

If anything, we usually pray just the opposite. Yet even though I hold some differing theological beliefs from these writers, I can't help believing that they were on to something life-changing. How would the world be different today if more Christians prayed with that kind of integrity? I mean, they are only saying what we all know to be true. It reflects a level of honesty and trust not seen very often today.

These prayers certainly do not reflect the modern philosophy that we should avoid speaking of sin and its effects if we wish to win people to Christ. After all, we don't want to turn people off of the gospel by dwelling too much on sin. It is a real downer. Right? We can't expect to draw crowds by reminding them of how "toadlike" they are! Tell that to John Owen, author of *Of the Mortification of Sin in Believers* or to Richard Sibbes with his most loved writing *The Bruised Reed*. Both of these books are puritan classics written specifically on the subject of overcoming our sin natures. These are two of many.

Now, I must say this. We must also read such things through the eyes of historical accuracy. Many of these same people and the cultures in which they lived were somewhat legalistic in their beliefs and behaviors. I am not advocating that at all. The church of their period had many flaws, of which legalism was definitely one. That much is certain. And yes, Jesus had much to teach on the dangers of legalism. Nevertheless, in spite of this, these writers had a confidence and assurance in their faith that we do not see often today. Their recognition of their sin did not seem to lead to defeat, but to a calm assurance and peace.

Go further back than the Puritans, all the way back to Augustine or earlier, and you will see it too. Augustine's *Confessions* is believed to be the world's oldest autobiography. It is really more of a testimony to his own sinfulness and alternately God's saving grace. Augustine knew just how capable he was of evil and sin. He understood what Paul meant in Romans 7:21 when he said, "I find then a law, that, when I would do good, evil is present with me." As a result, Augustine also knew just how much God loved him in spite of it.

You see, Augustine and others like him were confident in their salvation. Yet seen alongside that confidence in God is their lack of confidence in themselves. They knew that left to their own devices, they would most likely choose sin over righteousness almost every time. Admitting this weakness made them stronger.

Paul, too, set such an example in scripture. Paul considered himself not only a "wretched man" but also the "chiefest of sinners" (1 Tim. 1:15). This understanding of himself came over times as he matured in his faith. In 1 Corinthians 15:9, Paul referred to himself as the "least of the apostles." Sometime later, after maturing and growing in wisdom and faith, that self-description evolved into the "chiefest of sinners." He went from considering himself a lesser apostle to thinking himself the greatest of sinners. The more he understood of the Lord and the closer he got to him, the more of his old man nature he also recognized in himself.

Further, we see any gambit of emotions in Paul's writings. We see love. We see affection. We see frustration with others. We see anger. We see all sorts of human emotions. In his Romans 7 rant, we see frustration with himself. But one thing we do not see anywhere is a lack of confidence in his faith, in his salvation or in his Savior. So much so that he could write Philippians, the epistle of joy, from a prison cell.

So what does this teach me? It teaches me that it is possible to have a healthy grasp of my dirtiness and not be turned away from Christ. In fact, it may be just the opposite. Acknowledging my proneness to sin may actually draw me closer to Jesus. Coming to grips with Jesus's teaching that "apart from me you can do nothing" in John 15:5, actually serves to bring us closer to him. Knowing my weaknesses not only helps me defend myself against possible temptations, but it also increases my appreciation for what Jesus has done for me. After all, if he can love me with all my sins, then he must really love me. I mean really, really love me... It is not just some superficial self-serving love. It is a love above all others. No one else on Earth can honestly say that they would love me no matter what.

Even those closest to me would only put up with so much. Yet that is exactly what Jesus does. He loves us no matter what we do.

Okay. So let's time travel back to today. Are we really any different than those monks or Puritans from church history? No. Look back to those Puritan prayers, and you will see these sinners struggling with the same things we do today. Pride. Selfishness. Envy. Laziness. Lust. Earlier than that, likewise, Augustine struggled greatly with lust. Surprise! That particular sin didn't begin with the creation of the internet. It has been plaguing mankind since creation. Nothing has changed with human nature since the very beginning. From the Garden of Eden forward, we have all been sinners. No person is left out, and no sin is left out.

And guess what? Even born-again believers still have that old nature with which to struggle. It doesn't go away just because we come to Christ.

The difference between the believer's and nonbeliever's struggles with the old man is that born-again believers now have a new nature from which they can choose to listen too over the old one. As Paul would teach in Romans 6:6, we're no longer slaves to the old man nature. We no longer have to go along with our old man nature and its leadings. The old man is not who we are anymore. We can choose the new man over the old. We'll look at this more later.

So what does that choice lead too? You already know. That is probably why you're reading this book. Here comes the struggle. Here comes the man-in-the-mirror moments. Here comes the… *crrrrooooak*!

And if not handled properly, here comes the discouragement.

What must we do to move from this discouragement to the confidence of these heroes of the faith?

Well, for the purpose of this chapter, one of the first things we can do is simple. Do not be surprised by your sinfulness. Don't expect more of yourself than that which God expects. God knows you. He knows what you are capable of, good and bad.

An extremely telling verse is one found in Psalm 103. It is verse 14. It reads, "For He himself knows our frame; He is mindful that we are but dust." In other words, God knows what we are made of, both literally and spiritually.

God knows that you deal with depression by overeating.

God knows that you are too proud to admit you need help with an addiction.

God knows that you have often sought affirmation through inappropriate physical human relationships.

God knows what you have erased from your browser history.

God knows how bad you feel after you lose your temper…again.

God knows about your past.

God knows…he really does.

But here is the good news. He still loves you!

The verse prior to the Psalm 103:14 made from dust verse reads, "Just as a father has compassion on his children, So the Lord has compassion on those that fear Him." This is important. This life-changing biblical truth is that God knows you as you are and loves you as you are. It's as if we think somehow our faults come as a surprise to God, as if he didn't know what we were going to do when he first saved us. Of course, he knew then just as he knows now. That is why he saved us! He knew we couldn't save ourselves. It is a reality we must face, and it is a liberating reality.

Have you ever contemplated as to why Jesus tells us in Luke 9:23 to "take up our cross daily"? Why didn't he just say "take up your cross"? Why the *daily*? Why wasn't taking up our cross once on the day of our conversion enough? Is it because he knew that each new day would bring brand-new sins? Yes. Is it because he knew we are *still* sinners? Yes. Remember, He knows of what we are made. Also keep this in mind. He saved us from the penalty and power of sin, not the presence of it. Not yet at least. But that reality does not change a thing about what we know to be true of the Gospel message.

He died for my sins. All of them.

He loved the whole world. All of us.

He wants a relationship with everyone…even the toads!

We will continue to look at this more in the remaining chapters. But for now, know that recognizing my own proneness to sin doesn't mean I should be content to continue in sin. In fact, I would say it is impossible. Someone who has truly been born again will be miserable in continued sin. That is the discontent we see with the man-in-the-mirror moments. That's the disgust we feel at our own shortcomings. That is the wretchedness. It's miserable. But it is not a misery that has to lead to defeat. It is meant to be a reminder of the great love of our Savior. Let it remind you that you are loved no matter what. Facing this reality is to help us overcome and it will help you as you fight the discouragement.

We do not overcome all at once. We overcome a little each day as we take up our cross anew. Then one day, when we stand before our Lord, we will have overcome once and for all. That is the good news of the Gospel. So don't give in to defeat. Today, you may still be a toad. One day, it will be different. But for now, just know it is nothing out of the ordinary. You are not alone. You are not the only frog in the room. We all have warts. You may be broken, but not beyond his repair. He knew that when he paid for you by going to the cross.

I believe those Puritan brothers and sisters were on to something very profound. Don't turn away from the mirror. Look into it. Thank God for it. Ask God for it. God's word is a mirror (James 1:23–25). God's Holy Spirit conviction is a mirror.

Each time you look into it with honest eyes, you slowly chip away at the power of the old man to control you. Each time you look into it with honest eyes, knowing there is nothing you can do to change it, you give God an opportunity to work. Each time you look into it with honest eyes, you will see more and more of Jesus working in you. The more you see your sinful bent, the more amazing God's grace becomes. Do not run from it. Anticipate it. Expect it. Prepare for it. After all, you cannot kill the old man if you don't first acknowledge he is in the room.

"Where sin increased, grace abounds all the more" (Rom. 5:20 NASB).

Looking Even Deeper

Personal/Group Discussion and Application

1. Read Romans 5:19–21.

2. In Romans 5:20, Paul says that the law came so that the transgression might increase. How can God's law cause our sinfulness to increase? What does this imply for every believer familiar with the law and word of God?

3. Many people, believers and nonbelievers alike, are often quick to equate being a Christian with being a "good" person. Why do we have this tendency and why can it be discouraging?

4. Do you agree with the author's statement "He saved us from the penalty and power of sin, not the presence of it"? What evidence do you have for this answer?

5. How does the statement "Do not be surprised by your sinfulness" make you feel? Why?

6. Why do we need grace to abound even more as stated in Romans 5:21?

7. Pray asking God to let his grace abound in your heart more and more every day.

3

The Pain of Grace

Quia amasti me, fecisti me amabilem.
(In loving me, you made me lovable.)
— St. Augustine

And from his fullness we have all received, grace upon grace.
— John 1:16 (ESV)

This is the chapter I almost omitted. I wanted to omit it. Yet with pride swallowed, here it is. I hope you take it with the spirit intended.

In the beginning chapters of this book, I spoke of my man-in-the-mirror moments and the inevitability of that self-realization if indeed I wish to put away my old man. Well, I must admit that spiritual epiphanies like those are sometimes slow in coming to me. It is ironic really, in that, I spend so much time in the studying of God's word. I mean, after all, that's what pastor's do, isn't it? Aren't pastors supposed to have some special connection with God that allows them to grasp spiritual truths faster and at a more regular rate than other believers? (Again, imagine me somewhat self-righteously patting myself on the back... Thank you.)

Well, I hate to give away a secret I share with my fellow laborers of vocational ministry, but the truth is that, we are no different than anyone else when it comes to our relationship with God. We are only as close as we strive to be. In fact, I would take it a step further and say that we are in a more vulnerable position than most; in that, we can get so caught up in doing "ministry" and developing an environment that facilitates life-changing experiences for others, that we miss the simple truths that God is showing *us* along the way in our everyday goings-on. We can get so involved in the work of the church and her people that we miss the work he is doing in our own often neglected hearts and families. Put simply, His providential hand becomes every day and ordinary to the point that we can't see it as we once did. It is at best a tricky balance to maintain. Nevertheless, it does often happen that minister's share the same struggles of everyone else and that we too can sometimes miss God's grace at work in front of our faces.

For me, I was in a spiritual funk. I had been in one for several years, and I was admittedly a little slow on the uptake when it came to spiritual epiphanies, or as I prefer to call them, growth moments. I needed one badly. I wouldn't know just how badly until after it happened.

Now before you jump to a wrong conclusion about what I am saying here, I am not speaking of some form of special revelation apart from scripture. I am instead referring to one of those God-given moments when his word, which I have always trusted as being unarguably true, becomes *my* truth. It becomes personal when God uses his "two-edged sword" of Hebrews 4:12 and using a Holy Spirit-guided cut, slices right down to the marrow of my spiritual ignorance and apathy, and the resulting outcome is personal growth. I have been fileted in this manner more than once in my life.

For now, however, God was going to have to do something really drastic to snap me out of my deep spiritual complacency and into a healthier grasp of what following him truly means. And drastic it would be. I will leave the existential question as to whether it was God or whether God just used the situation for his purposes to your own personal pondering. But I do know this much for certain. Something happened in my life that grabbed my attention with a vice grip determination, and my God was definitely and intimately involved with me through it all.

It happened on a June early summer day a few years ago. My eyes were forced opened to what I am calling the pain of grace.

It was early in the morning. An eighteen-year-old young man entered my home at approximately 6:30 a.m. When I approached him, he let vent his rage against the world, and he attacked me. He pounced on me like a wild animal, knocking me to the ground, landing me with great force upon my kitchen floor with him perched upon my chest on his knees. He then began to punch me repeatedly about my face and head for what to me seemed like a fuzzy almost dreamlike forever. Then after I finally managed to block some of the blows coming toward my face, he then wrapped his fingers around my throat and began squeezing to the point that I could not breathe or speak. All the while he was banging my head against the hard tile floor. He finally broke free for a moment out of his rage enough to let up on his python grip to my throat, and I was able to push back with some success. I jumped to my feet and started running away only to have him chase me and start again hitting the back of my head. Finally, his rage subsided, and he stopped hitting and cursing and he darted out the front door of my house and down the street.

My face had been split and was bleeding profusely, and our kitchen looked like a murder had taken place. My blood was all over the floor and walls of our white kitchen. Then my teenage son and ten-year-old son emerged along with my wife to witness the aftermath of this senseless attack. Thankfully, my teenage and very much "daddy's girl" daughter had been out of town this week and did not witness firsthand the immediate aftereffect of this misguided rage. I walked away with concussions, countless scratches and cuts, a broken nose and finger, and a damaged retina in my right eye. To say the least, it would be an event that would literally shake the foundations of my family's faith and sense of security.

I struggled with whether or not I should include the details of this account in this book. After much prayer and heart-to-heart conversation with family, I discovered that it is so vital a part our journey of faith that to do otherwise would be to neglect an opportunity for growth for all involved. In other words, I felt I must.

I am sure as you read of this nightmare experience, you are probably as disturbed by the possibility of something like this happening as much as me. An assault like this in our home is unthinkable. Yet it happened and does happen more than you might think. This I learned the hard way.

You see, there are still more variables to the story I have yet to tell you before you jump to conclusions. It gets even more complicated.

Would it change your opinion of the attacker if I told you that he had been earlier diagnosed with bipolar disorder? Would it change your mind about him if I told you that he had just finished a seven-month stay in a mental health facility and was just released two months prior to this event and that it was his third such hospitalization? Would it change your opinion if you knew he had not been taking his medication?

Okay. It probably would. And it probably should. But here is the clincher.

Would it change your thoughts on this event if I told you that this young man was my son?

Because he is. He is my oldest son, and I love him more than I can express in words.

So you see, it is more than just a story of an assault of my physical person. This was an assault on my very heart. It was an assault on my family and my identity as father, husband, pastor, and friend. And it was an assault on my son. It called the last eighteen years of my life into question, and even as I stood there on my front steps in front of police officers, paramedics, and neighbors covered in my own blood, I knew my life and that of my family would never again be the same.

As shocking as this may seem to you, it was not an all-at-once surprise for us. In fact, I can honestly say that once the physical struggle was over, there was a part of me that even as I bled felt relieved that it had finally happened. I was relieved that the inevitable had occurred and that I was the only one that had been hurt. I also felt relief in the thought that in spite of how bad it had been, it could have been so much worse. No permanent physical damage had taken place aside from a tiny scar above my right eye. A little glue here and there, some Band-Aids, cold packs, and painkillers; and in time, I would be as good as new…at least physically.

It was not a surprise for us, though, in that we had been living with this disorder for several years, though most would not have known it; in that, we did a fairly good job of hiding it. It had really begun to materialize around the age of twelve or thirteen for my son. It was then that we began to see a transformation in his personality. He had morphed from a carefree, fun-loving young boy to a troubled and aggressively angry teen. He had begun to exhibit fits of rage along the way and became increasingly threatening in his manner. We've made more trips to the emergency room than I can count to mend his self-inflicted damage to his hand from his punching walls and/or trees when he would get angry. He had stolen, lied, run away, and disrespected and disrupted our family in almost every way imaginable. We had to have police at our home many times to simply help calm him and to protect him from himself and these types of dramatic occurrences had intensified and multiplied.

We had been anticipating that ultimately this disorder would come to a head and someone would be hurt in spite of all the steps we had taken to get him help over the years. We had even relocated multiple times over the years, leaving home and ministries behind, much to the detriment of our careers, hoping that a fresh start and new friends would make a difference in his life. As parents who cared beyond explanation for their son and in spite of all our efforts, his mom and I could see that his inner demons were gaining ground in his soul. It was evident that a climactic encounter was inevitable. For some time, we had lived in a certain level of fear. At least now, the walking-on-eggshells lifestyle we had all developed around him would have a reprieve. Perhaps now, he could get the help he needs.

So as bad as it was, we could now breathe a little.

Yet how do you describe what we were feeling beyond that? It is almost impossible. How do you explain the fact that you have been hurt by someone you love so deeply? How do you keep loving someone that under different circumstances might have killed you that day? Even more so, how do you keep loving someone that keeps hurting you? Many of you have the same questions. It seems impossible. But I promise you, it is not.

In the days that followed the incident, few people knew how to express their sorrow to us for the pain we were experiencing. It was such an awkward thing to talk about. Even now, I find it difficult and so do those around me. Thankfully, God had brought me to a body of believers at Macedonia Community Baptist Church that loved on us through it all. They poured their love out on their pastor and family and on our son in numerous ways. Through them I had now learned much of what it means to be part of a church family from the care *receiver's* point of view. I will never forget what big love this small congregation shared with us during what was unmistakably the darkest hour of my life.

It was never more evident than on the following Sunday. To make this whole scenario even worse, the coming Sunday following the assault was Father's Day. I am not sure if I made the right decision or not, but after some encouragement from a godly man in my congregation and after much thought, I agreed that it was important that my church family see me that day and I grew determined to not let Satan have a victory that Sunday by keeping me home. So I went to church and preached a Father's Day message with black and swollen eyes, broken fingers, very noticeable knots all over my head and face, a crooked nose, bandages, braces, and a muscle stiffness that made it difficult to even walk to the pulpit. In my Father's Day "inspirational" service, I had to explain to my congregation how my son had beaten me up just a few days prior and that he was now in jail. There was not a dry eye in the place. I think it was safe to say that it was an unforgettable Father's Day sermon.

As I shared before the service my reluctance to be there with the aforementioned godly man that had encouraged me to come, he told me that he was so thankful I came. He reassured me that my church needed to see that I was okay and then told me that by being there "I gave the devil a black eye" that morning. I am not sure of the theology of that statement, but I love the sentiment.

The next few months would be a series of family counseling, lawyers, district attorneys, judges, and video visitation with our son. It was finally determined that he needed extensive and legally mandated help and thankfully the system worked to that end. We still had a long way to go.

Hope still prevailed. We never gave up on him and still to this day pray for his healing. There have been times of progress and times of setback that would still take place. We have grown closer, and then we've had moments of distance. Like us all, he still has the old man of his sinful nature to wrestle. Sometimes he wins. Sometimes he loses. His battle is still raging.

While I never wish to repeat anything even remotely similar to any of this, I do feel as if I have grown as a result. I do not say that in any self-serving kind of way. Trust me, there are easier ways to learn. Nevertheless, through it all, I did learn something and it is my desire to share with you what I have learned.

If I could sum up what I have learned through all of this, it would be that there is sometimes a painful aspect to grace.

Let's consider what I mean by that.

First, I would like to say that the lesson ended there. I cannot. For almost four years from the day of that incident, our family underwent a series of trials the likes of which I hope to never repeat. In addition to all we went through trying to help our son and get him to a place of peace in his own heart, we all experienced even more upheaval. We had other issues with some of our other children; we had a series of serious health issues, including three major surgeries for my wife, including open-heart surgery. I had heart issues, cancer, several surgeries, and other health issues. My father has had health issues. As a bivocational pastor, I had job transitions that took place in the midst of all of it. We had financial struggles as a result of this and other problems. Put simply, for almost four years, we moved desperately from one trial to the next.

And through it all, I have to admit something. I was beginning to think that maybe God was punishing me for something. In the back of my mind, I was literally translating disappointment within myself and doubts of my parenting and pastoring abilities into an explanation for why I was going through all of this. After all, I must be getting punished because no one else had ever experienced anything like this…

Wrong.

The pain I was experiencing is common to all. My pain was no worse than anyone else's. It just so happened that my life had been virtually pain free up until this incident. Then it came upon us all of a sudden. It was overwhelming.

This is especially true concerning the pain I was experiencing where the aforementioned son was concerned. I wanted to help him. I wanted to be with him. Some days, I was angry with him. Other days, I was angry with myself. My emotions were all over the place. I didn't know how to feel.

But in the midst of it, I remembered a prayer I had prayed not long before all of this began. I had prayed asking God to help me better understand the concept of grace. Dear Lord, give me an understanding of grace. Boy, did he…

I had read every book I could get in my hands on the subject of grace. It was easy for me in the beginning because I worked in a Christian bookstore. I had easy access. So I collected every writing I could find specifically on the subject of the grace of God. But nothing I read had the impact of experiencing what I did with my son. It was the best teacher I could have had on the subject of grace.

Now please do not infer from this that I am saying God caused all of this to happen to teach me a lesson on grace. I do not believe any of this happened because God wanted it too. It happened because we live in a fallen world. Sickness happens because our bodies are touched by sin and death. So does mental illness. What happened with my son was no one's fault per say. It, too, was a result of living in a fallen world where mental disorders exist. He is no different from you or I or any other person that walks this Earth. He has got his old man nature constantly there to confuse him as we all do. Sometimes he listens, other times he does not. But at the end of the day, he is a sinner like everyone else.

Immediately after the incident, as I began sharing with loved ones and church family what had been going on in our family, I began to hear story after story of others dealing with similar stories of mental illness, rebellious children, and any variety of family issues. For the first time since I had been in the ministry, I was now truly qualified to speak to people on the subject, and suddenly, I realized how many hearts have been through similar trials. It was amazing. It was overwhelming. And it was humbling. God was using it to start conversations I probably never would have had otherwise. He seems to specialize in taking what our enemy means for bad and using it for good.

But the more I had these conversations, the more I remembered that prayer. Teach me about grace. Help me understand grace. What was I thinking? Uhh… Lord, I meant receiving grace, not showing grace to others. I'll be clearer next time…

What I learned, however, was that it was one thing to receive grace, another to give it. And maybe the lesson for me was if I wanted to better understand how amazing God's grace really is to receive, I first needed to understand what it means to give it away. And for us mere mortals, it can sometimes hurt. It involves denying yourself the pleasure of seeing a wrong made right.

I was angry with what had happened. I was angry with my son. I was angry with myself. I was angry with so many things. Yet at the same time, what I wanted more than anything was to have my son back in my life. I knew for that to happen, I had to forgive him. Anyone with a prodigal knows exactly what I am talking about. You want to hug their necks and at the same time pinch their heads off. I would learn that it is possible to be angry and not want to offer forgiveness and yet still love someone beyond measure. I wanted to forgive him. Yet I also wanted him to show remorse for what he had done. I wanted him back, yet I wanted him to feel the consequences.

I knew what I was supposed to do and what would ultimately be best for him, but at the same time, I wasn't sure I wanted to do it. Yet in time, I did. I forgave him and welcomed him back into my life. At first, it hurt. It meant basically pushing my feelings to the side in favor of reconciliation. There were days when it just did not feel fair after what I had been through. But I am so glad I did it. I learned that grace has nothing to do with fairness. That is what makes it so valuable.

Now the pain is gone, and I enjoy his presence and that of the grandson he has provided me. And I had to allow it never knowing if he would ever understand what it was like for me. He would eventually do his part to make it right again, and for that, I am so proud. But I had to forgive him, not knowing if that would ever happen. After all, the Bible does not mince words on how we are to forgive others. I knew I had to forgive…whether he would ever deserve it or not.

Which raises the question, do any of us deserve grace?

If we did, it wouldn't be grace. Grace is the *undeserved, unmerited* favor of God. It has nothing to do with whether or not we deserve it. It is entirely God's gift. It is forgiveness when we haven't asked for it. It is love shown when we have not given love. It is a hug instead of the slap in the face we deserve. It is running toward those that have wronged you instead of running away. It is grace.

Perhaps what has become one of my favorite Bible verses of all time is found in the gospel of Luke in the midst of what is considered by many as the most beloved of all parables. It is the story of the prodigal son. I prefer the language of the King James Version for this verse. It is Luke 15:20. It reads: "And he arose, and came to his father. But when he was yet a great way off, his father saw him, and had compassion, and ran, and fell on his neck, and kissed him."

He fell on his neck and kissed him. I love that! What a picture that description paints.

Contained within this one verse, we see the very heart of our God. We see in the person of the father a representation of our Heavenly Father. The father in the story not only forgives his son, but he is looking for him while he was still a "great way off." Then instead of waiting for him to return, he hikes up his robes, and I'm guessing in a very undignified way runs out to meet him. You also know the rest of the story. Upon meeting him, he throws a big party and welcomes him home, much to the chagrin of his other son.

The back story that makes this reunion so special is what this son had done to his father. Think about it. He had basically told him that I don't want to be with you anymore. I just want you to give me what I have coming to me, as if he was somehow owed an inheritance instead of it being a gift. To make it worse, he was not willing to wait for his inheritance. He wanted it now. He had plans which did not involve staying home and obeying his father. It was as if his son had said to him, "You can't tell me what to do anymore. Just give me your money and leave me alone. I'm tired of listening to you. I want to do my own thing." He was done with it. He was done with this life. Done with this family. It could not have been a worse insult for someone in that time and culture. For that matter, it would be just as bad today. Put yourself in that position.

Imagine how much it must have hurt the father. Imagine the pain he felt as he gave into his son and watched him ride away much too soon in life with half of his belongings, not knowing if he would ever see him again. He was probably within his rights as a father in that time period to have his son stoned for this behavior. But in Jesus's story he refrained from taking legal and ethical revenge. Instead of punishment, he simply let him go.

Out of love, he allowed his son to make a huge mistake. That's grace.

Out of love for his son, he allowed him to insult and humiliate him for all to see. Grace.

Out of love for his son, he unnecessarily suffered great loss. Grace.

And out of love for his son, he welcomed him back unconditionally with open arms. Grace.

I have always imagined that his other son was not the only person to complain about the manner in which the father invited the son back home with open arms. There were probably many telling him how he should discipline the young man. There are always well-meaning friends ready and willing to tell you how to handle a situation the likes of which they have never dealt. Believe me, I know. So does anyone who has ever been through a crisis.

But you can see why that verse is so beautiful to me. The father, in defiance of the advice he was probably given and the fatherly instinct he was probably feeling, ran out to meet his long-lost son and then fell on his neck and kissed him. The phrase "fell on his neck" is best translated "kept kissing him." He grabbed him and kept kissing him.

To the father, it was a reason to celebrate. His son had been lost. Now he was found. He didn't stop to ask the boy if he had learned his lesson. He didn't rebuke him for spending all his wealth on wild parties and wild women. No. He just kept kissing him. Then he wanted everyone else to join in with him in the celebration.

For the father to be able to do that, he had to push aside his pride. He had to allow others to talk. He had to listen to others say things like "that boy doesn't deserve that" or "If I was you, I wouldn't let him back into your life." At best, I am sure there were others willing to do as the prodigal had expected and just let him come back as a servant and work off his debt. The father would have been within his rights to do that. Even his son knew that. He was probably more surprised than anyone by his father's acceptance.

For the father to do what he did, he had to push everything aside that his instincts were probably telling him to do. That is the human father of the story. For him, showing grace to his son would come with a price. For him, perhaps it would mean sacrificing his own will, his own dignity, and his own reputation. It would be painful. Yet to him, it must have been worth the pain to get his son back. He would have to feel the pain of grace in order to get his son back.

Now for our heavenly Father, whom Jesus qualitatively represents in this story with an earthly father, his grace also came with a price. For our heavenly father to get you and me back, he would also have to make a sacrifice. For him, it would be his own Son on the cruel cross of Calvary.

Get you and I back? Are we prodigals? I say yes. Yes, we are. Or at least we were at one point in our lives. Whenever we choose to listen to the old man nature and follow its leading, we are doing just as the prodigal in that story did. We are saying to our heavenly father that "I want to do my own thing. I'm tired of doing what you say."

For you and I to be welcomed back in the same style as the son of the story, the cost of the party, the cost of our disobedience all had to be put on our Father's account. Why? Because just like the boy in that story who found himself eating out of a pig trough and longing for home, we have absolutely nothing to offer. We are wretched, remember? There is nothing I could do to win back the favor of my heavenly Father. Only grace would cover me.

And for that to happen, our heavenly Father had to experience the pain of grace.

To be clear, do not take that statement to mean that our heavenly father was not willing to do it. When I talk about the pain of grace, I do not wish to infer that God had to swallow his pride in order to provide us with salvation. Pride is sinful. God does not sin. But I do believe God experiences pain.

The bible speaks of God the Father being grieved by our actions and rebellions as well as the Holy Spirit being grieved. See Genesis 6:6, Psalm 78:40, Isaiah 63:10, and others and follow the biblical references. You will see that it is possible to hurt God by our rejection of him. That grief exists because he has such a deep longing for intimacy with his children. He has gone to great lengths to provide the means by which we can obtain that intimacy, even to the sacrifice of the cross. To reject it is the worst insult we could offer. It's even worse than the rejection of the prodigal in that story. Yes, God grieves.

With that grief, though, we must also remember that Christ considered it a *joy* to endure the cross. Read Hebrews 12:2: "Looking unto Jesus the author and finisher of *our* faith; who for the joy that was set before him endured the cross, despising the shame, and is set down at the right hand of the throne of God."

Jesus considered it a joy to die for us. Not that it was a joy to suffer, but that it was a joy to suffer *for us*. Why? Because to him, you were worth the pain of grace.

I don't think it was until I experienced what I did with my son that I fully grasped just how deep God's love is for me. To love someone who at times loves you and at other times prefers to rebel is not easy. I would say there is no pain any worse. I think it would be easier to just have someone straight up hate you than to have someone that you know loves you turn against you. Yet even though that is how I felt about my son, I did love him and always will. I would do anything to restore and keep our relationship in place, no matter the pain.

Is our heavenly Father any different? His love is greater than mine; therefore, his desire for reconciliation must be greater as well. It must break his omnipotent heart on an omnipotent level when we choose to reject or at best ignore his sacrifice and love.

It must grieve the very heart of God every time we choose to listen to the old man instead of following the new nature for which he gave his Son so that we might follow. And not only follow, but follow for our own good. When we as believers choose to go with that old nature, it must be like saying to our heavenly father, "Just give me my inheritance and leave me alone." It has to break his heart. I know I have broken his heart and caused him pain many times. That reality brings me to this life-changing conclusion: He must really love me. We are not talking about some superficial, fair-weather kind of love. It means he must love me with an all-powerful can't get enough of me never wanting to be apart from me kind of love.

To endure the pain of the cross, the pain of grace for me, he must passionately love me. And if he loves me that much, there's probably nothing I can do to cause him to feel any different toward me. From the Garden of Eden forward, God has had one driving purpose. Reconciliation. The reconciliation of our relationships with him has been his heartbeat. And he did it all for me.

When I think about what happened with my son, I can't help but see my own sinfulness. He is no different than any of us. My son's old man nature is constantly nagging at him, taunting him, teasing him, and tempting him. His spirit is at war with his flesh. He has the same choice to make as all of us. I am no different. Under different circumstances, who is to say I would not have done the same thing? I cannot say. But I can say this. I am so thankful that God was willing to run after sinful me, to meet me fresh out of the pigpen and to fall on my neck with kiss after kiss.

Now what does this realization do for us? It sets us free.

Some might call this an easy grace or a cheap grace. I say there was nothing cheap or easy about it. Some would agree with the brother and say that the sinful son does not deserve to be restored. Guess what. They are right. He does not. Neither do you or me. That is why God's grace is so beautiful.

That is also why the proper response to grace and especially knowing the pain of grace, is not to sin more, but to sin less. Sinning more is probably what the brother and many others probably thought would happen in the story. But when you truly get what is being done for you, there is a desire to live for the giver of grace, not to live against him. The pain of grace becomes a sin deterrent.

Will I always be successful over the old man nature? Probably not. I will most likely cause the Lord more pain along the way. The verse of Romans 5:20 I gave at the end of chapter 2 addresses this, however. Where sin increases…grace abounds even more. You see, when I fail, he just gives more grace. But this truth doesn't invite more sinfulness as we might suspect. Paul addresses this in Romans 6:1–2. He basically asks if we are to sin more so that we can receive more grace. "May it never be," he says.

If we truly comprehend what has been done for us, knowing the pain of grace means that more than ever I will long to choose to listen to the new nature over the old. Once you grasp the depth of God's love and grace, you do not wish to cause him more pain. You wish only to live for and be with your heavenly Father. The pain of grace is what makes it so special. It is not cheap or easy. It is priceless.

In conclusion, one more weapon to use in the killing of your old man, to putting away that old nature and in stopping those reoccurring habits that plague your mental well-being is to remember that the grace God has shown you has come with a great price tag. It cost Jesus the pain of the cross. It cost our heavenly Father the pain of watching it. He was willing and did it with joy because of his love for dirty old you. It is the pain of grace. Don't take it for granted. Don't wait for an experience like mine to understand it.

As for our family, our lives have somewhat stabilized for now. Our health is fine. Our relationships are all fine and we are all looking forward to the future. God's grace brought us through it all. I would take nothing for the experience because of what I have learned; though, I certainly hope to never have to repeat any of it. But if I do, I know the grace of God will meet my greatest needs. The pain of grace for me was a teaching pain. And as a result, if I do go through something like this again, the old man nature will have less of a say in how I handle things. Reflecting on the pain of grace has weakened my old man.

To kill the old man, one must make reflecting on God's grace part of your everyday life. Jerry Bridges, author of *Holiness Day by Day*, instructed us in that book to "[p]reach the Gospel to yourself every day." That is good advice from a fellow struggler. Think on it every day. Cherish the gospel for the treasure it is. Cherish grace for the treasure it is. Cherish the pain of grace.

Looking Even Deeper

Personal/Group Discussion and Application

1.   Read Luke 15:11–32.

2.   What feelings do you experience when reading the story of the prodigal son?

3.   How can you relate to the son, the father, and the brother in the story of the prodigal?

4.   Have you or someone close to you ever experienced a personal crisis similar to the one the author shared in this chapter? If so, how did you respond those involved? What did God teach you through this situation?

5.   In your own words, what is the pain of grace?

6.   How important is understanding the "pain of grace" to you in helping us overcome our sinful nature? Why?

7.   Pray thanking God for his grace and ask him to help you never to take his grace for granted.

4

Here Be Dragons

> Jesus did not identify the person with his sin, but rather saw in this
> sin something alien, something that really did not belong to him,
> something that merely chained and mastered him and from which
> he would free him and bring him back to his real self. Jesus was able
> to love men because he loved them right through the layer of mud.
>
> —Helmut Thielicke

> For the mind set on the flesh is death, but the mind set
> on the Spirit is life and peace, because the mind set on
> the flesh is hostile toward God; for it does not subject
> itself to the law of God, for it is not even able to do so;
> and those who are in the flesh cannot please God.
>
> —Romans 8:6–8 (NASB)

On some ancient and archaic maps, the words "Here be dragons" or "There be dragons" appear scribbled in the corners or along the edges. Of course, it is doubtful that the original cartographer actually believed there were literal dragons in that location. It was most likely a way for them to convey the uncertainty of what lies ahead on that uncharted portion of the map. Or perhaps it was a creative way to warn the explorer from venturing into what was known to be dangerous territory. It may have been dangerous waters, treacherous land masses, unknown wildlife, or even hostile natives. The dragon warning was for the protection of those that followed the map. It was not necessarily expressing belief on the part of the mapmaker in a giant fire breathing lizard. It was a warning sign for real-life dangers ahead.

Well, with that said, I feel I must warn you. When it comes to our exploration of our own human heart... Here be dragons!

In his classic Christian writing *The Mortification of Sin in Believers*, puritan writer John Owen describes the human heart as the "habitation of dragons." He is, of course, referring to the inclination of the human heart to sin and evil. He was affirming the old nature man-in-the-mirror revelation we have been discussing. He saw it in himself, and he saw it in others. After all, as much as we might wish to extol human virtue and benevolence, it only takes a peripheral look around to notice that yes, the human heart can be a dark and foul place, a habitat for dragons. All forms of corruption take place daily, even from what we would consider "good" people. It is unfortunate, but true.

Further reading in that classic treatise on the reality and severity of sin in the heart of a believer, reveals that the dragons he is referring to are the usual temptations and proclivity for sin that we all deal with in our hearts. He speaks of lusts and envies and the like. I would like to take it a step further, however. I want us to consider two specific dragons. One of these dragons comes from within and the other from without.

The first and probably the most dangerous dragon that inhabits our heart is the dragon of self. I say it is the most dangerous because it is at the heart of almost every other fight we have within our own hearts. I would say that self is the motive behind every sin we commit and by default behind every one of those shameful self-loathing man-in-the-mirror not-again moments. This dragon is formidable.

Of course, John Owens's understanding of the dragon-infested human heart came from his understanding of the Word of God and from personal real-life experience. Self is a topic of much discussion in the scriptures. Specifically, let's consider Paul's words from Romans 6–8. The theme of dangerously inappropriate self-love permeates the scriptures, both the Old and the New Testament. But Paul attacks this dragon head on in these three chapters from Romans. He doesn't always use the word *self*, however. More times than not, he uses the word *flesh*.

Our first thought when we hear the word *flesh* or *sins of the flesh* is to automatically think of the sin of lust, and then maybe if we are being super spiritual, the sin of gluttony. Though I must admit, not many in our day take the sin of gluttony too seriously. While these two sins definitely fit under the description of the flesh or sins of the flesh, it does not give us a full picture of what is meant by the word in scripture.

The flesh is more than just our physical bodies and all the temptations that accompany such a creation. The desires of the flesh do include sexual pleasure and physical ingratiation. It also includes, but is at the same time more than, coveting physical or material gain. However, what you can see, touch, or obtain is not all there is to the flesh. When Paul speaks of the flesh, he is talking about the self. He is addressing our desire to please our self, specifically to please our self even if to do so we must engage in acts of disobedience to God. Put simply, it is putting yourself before God.

This selfishness is at the heart of almost every other sin. For example, what is coveting if not wanting something for yourself that does not belong to you? What is lying if not an attempt to protect self or make yourself look better at the expense of others or your own integrity? What is gossip if not trying to curry favor for yourself in the eyes of others at the expense of someone not present? What is cheating or stealing if not an attempt to take and/or give yourself more of something that does not belong to you? What is the oft considered benign sin of sloth, if not putting feelings of self above your responsibilities? What is rejecting God's will for your life if not choosing self-will over God's? You see, every sin we can possibly commit, from committing murder or adultery to telling a little white lie can all be traced back to the dragon lair of self.

This has always been the case and will always be the case. Think back to the story of Eden. It was love of self that the serpent exploited to entice Eve and Adam to taste of the forbidden fruit. He told them basically that God didn't want them to taste it because God knows in that day, they eat from it "your eyes will be opened and you will be like God" (Gen. 3:5). In other words, eat this and even you can be as God, or perhaps you can even be your own God. Even you! He was a snake oil salesman from the beginning, deviously taking advantage of the battle in which we are all engaged. Even then, the battle within us would be the battle between the flesh and the Spirit.

Paul tells us in Romans 8:7 that the mind set on the flesh is hostile toward God. That means that the heart that puts self first is in actuality setting itself up as an enemy to God. To choose self is to choose the wrong side of the fight. This is important to remember. In fact, it is a necessary fact to remember if you wish to kill your old man nature and have victory over those besetting sins you struggle with repeatedly.

It is a hard truth for us to accept, though, isn't it? I think that is because we live in a culture where self-love is the norm. After all, we live in the "selfie" generation. This social promoting self-love we are bombarded with daily is an interesting phenomenon, but not a new one. Humanity has been self-centered from the dawn of creation. The difference is that the new technologies we have today with the phones, cameras, and social media make self-promotion and self-adoration so easy.

I can remember as a teenager receiving as a birthday present my first camera. It was a Polaroid, which was a brand-new and extremely advanced technology in its time. Yes, I know I am dating myself here. But I remember how I loved it. I mean, you could take a picture, and it would actually develop right there in front of you! It only took about five minutes! You just had to hold it by the corner and shake it and blow on it gently until the black shiny film began to morph into what was usually a cloudy, faded and amateurish-looking picture. But they were great! We could take a picture and have it in moments versus having to take your film down to the corner developer and waiting days or weeks to see the picture.

Now, however, we can take a picture, and instantly, it is uploaded to our social media accounts, and within minutes, it can be seen all over the world in high-definition crystal clarity. With this technology has come all the abuses and exploits you can imagine with such advancement. But at the heart of all of it is people promoting self, seeking self-endorsement, and pushing self-love at the expense of self-respect and dignity. This self-worshiping we see taking place in front of us is encouraged by many as simply a form of self-expression and extolled as self-confidence. I think the argument could be made that is the exact opposite of self-confidence. I see it as proof of a lack of self-confidence. That is why so many, especially young inexperienced and insecure people, put themselves out there for the whole world to see. By doing so, many are crying out for attention. They are trying to win the approval and admiration of others. Again, looking out for self, at any cost. For some, it is at the cost of their reputations and futures.

Oh, what a shame it is that more of us can't find satisfaction outside of ourselves! It certainly takes the pressure off living.

Again, it is not a new problem. It is just that these "advancements" have paved the way for the no holds barred self-gratifying behaviors. They enable the flesh, I would say, to the degrees of which mankind has never seen.

There is an ancient battle escalating between the flesh and spirit. The flesh often wins because we aren't taking seriously just how sinister it can be. It is our dragon.

Paul tells us in Galatians 5:16–18:

> But I say, walk by the Spirit, and you will not carry out the desire of the flesh. For the desire of the flesh is against the Spirit, and the Spirit against the flesh; for these are in opposition to one another, in order to keep you from doing whatever you want. But if you are led by the Spirit, you are not under the Law.

To not carry out the desires of the flesh, we must instead choose to walk by the Spirit. Again, it comes down to the idea that there are two natures at work. One we once belonged too and obeyed and a new one. No longer a slave to the old one, we no longer have to fulfill the desires of the flesh. We can now instead walk by the Spirit.

And walking by the Spirit releases us from the obligation of the flesh. Again, ultimately it comes down to a choice.

How do we walk by the Spirit?

If I could sum it up in one word, it would be this: *surrender*.

You walk by the Spirit by surrendering your "self" to him. You walk by the Spirit by spending your time with the Spirit, listening to the Spirit, and letting the Spirit guide you. We will look at some specifics in later chapters as we look at weapons of prayer, the Bible and worship and how we can use them in our struggle to kill the old man. But spending time doing these things means giving of your "self" to God. It is surrendering something of limited value, our time, for something of inestimable value. It only makes sense to surrender something that only means to harm us anyway in exchange for something that only wants to see us prosper and grow. Surrender is the exact opposite of selfishness. It is the giving up of self instead of taking for self. There is nothing more liberating than the spiritual act of surrender.

But for now, just know this. The dragon of self or the flesh is trying to set up housekeeping in your heart. He wants to be there because it was once his home. However, the dragon of self has experienced Holy Spirit eviction. Your heart is no longer his home. It belongs to the Spirit of God. However, that does not keep him from trying to make it his home. The flesh will try. Self will try. The old man will try. But rest assured, the Holy Spirit is not merely temporarily lodging in your heart, He lives there permanently. And he is greater than self.

Satisfying self is no longer your motivation. Pleasing God should be. If it is not the case, then perhaps you need to ask yourself if you are walking in step with the flesh or the Spirit. Are you walking in allegiance to the dragon or to the Holy Spirit of God? Have you surrendered those selfish fleshly struggles to the Lord or are you selfishly trying to overcome them by your own strength? Some would argue that even trying to overcome your sins by your own strength is in fact the old man trying to assert himself.

If you are trying to do it with pure self-determination, you will fail. In fact, that in and of itself is the very definition of living according to the flesh. You can't do it on your own. If we could slay the dragon of self on our own, we wouldn't need Jesus. You see, "you can do it yourself" is the primary lie of self. We can't do it on our own. The sooner you realize that, the sooner you will begin to see small victories over the self. Surrender is the key to victory. Ironic, huh? That is why Paul told us in 2 Corinthians 12:9–10 that he should really boast in his weaknesses because in them God's power is made perfect. Put simply, we have to get out of the way and let God fight for us. We have to surrender.

Yes, the dragon of self and flesh will be living in our shadows until the day our sins are once and for all slain for all time, until the day we are made perfect before God. Yes, the dragon of self will be a nuisance that we have to deal with from time to time. In some instances, he will be strong and almost impossible to resist. At others, he will be weak and less obvious a threat.

Just don't buy the lie the world would have you believe that the dragon of self is your friend. It is your enemy. The world teaches that self is good. In fact, right now it is teaching that self is everything. The truth is the exact opposite though. The love of self will cost you everything.

It was love of self that turned Lucifer, the most beautiful of all archangels in heaven, into a devil. It was also love of self that brought about the fall and eviction of mankind from paradise and brought sin and death into the world for all of us. The love of self will be your downfall as well. It will cost you everything. That is the lie of self-love. What starts as a desire to help yourself actually ends up causing its destruction. To truly help yourself, you must give yourself to the Lord.

Again, self is at the heart of this battle between the flesh and the Spirit, between the old man and the new creation. But thankfully your worth is not based on how others see you or how you perform. These are all lies of the dragon. Your worth is based on the fact that the all-mighty, all-powerful, all-loving God of the universe loved you enough to take upon himself *your* sins, just for the hopes of possibly having a relationship with you. You are good enough to be loved by God just as you are. That is who you really are.

If God were as we are, instead of selfies, he would be taking pictures of you and posting them. He loves you that much. Don't listen to the dragon of self. He is a liar. And if his voice sounds funny to you it is because the cross of Christ pulled the teeth of the dragon of self. He is powerless, unless you refuse to surrender to the Lord. In that case, self will rule the day.

Jesus told us in Luke 9:23, "And He was saying to *them* all, 'If anyone wants to come after Me, he must *deny* himself, take up his cross daily, and follow Me.'"

This denying of self is something we must do every day if we wish to truly follow Jesus. It is not a once and for all commitment. It is a daily recommitment. Remember what Paul told us in Romans 8:7–8 seen at the beginning of this chapter. The flesh cannot please God. It simply cannot. So don't try to manipulate it into being a source of godliness or goodness. Instead, simply deny it. Take up your cross daily and instead follow Jesus. That is how we kill the old man. That is how we slay the dragon of self.

Now, as I wrote earlier. The dragon of self is the dragon we must fight that comes from within. But there is another dragon, equally sinister. He comes from without. To kill our old man nature, we must prepare for battle against this dragon as well.

Looking Even Deeper

Personal/Group Discussion and Application

1. Read 2 Corinthians 12:7–10.

2. What do you think was Paul's thorn? Why?

3. In 2 Corinthians 12:9, we are told that "God's grace is sufficient for you, for power is perfected in weakness"? How does this play into our battle with our old man nature?

4. Do you agree with the author that self is at the heart of most, if not all sins? What evidence is there in your own life?

5. Why do we find it so hard to deny ourselves?

6. Pray asking God to bring to the surface your selfishness and give you the strength and desire to repent of it.

5

Adversary of My Soul

Satan, like a fisher, baits his hook according
to the appetites of the fish.
—Thomas Adams

If God were not my friend, Satan would not so much be my enemy.
—Thomas Brooks

And in your steadfast love you will cut off my enemies,
and you will destroy all the adversaries of my soul,
for I am your servant.
—Psalm 143:12 (ESV)

He is a liar. He is a deceiver. He would like nothing more than to see you fail. He is your enemy. The Bible tells us that he prowls around like a lion seeking whom he may devour (1 Pet. 5:8). He is the dragon from without mentioned in the previous chapter, and he wants to devour you. We fight not only against the dragon of self from within, but this enemy coming at us from outside ourselves. And he is fearsome and powerful.

While our enemy is not as powerful as our indwelling Savior and while he cannot take us as born-again believers to the hell that has been prepared for him and all his cohorts, he still has the capability of making our life on this Earth a temporary living hell. It is because of him that we not only have to fight against self and the flesh, but we also have to engage in spiritual warfare against forces of darkness and deception. These forces love to use our struggle with the old man nature to their advantage.

This is a reality that too many Christians seem to want to ignore and to their own demise. I feel it is the reason there are so many of us struggling with things like besetting sins and weak testimonies. It is because we have underestimated the reality of spiritual warfare. Living on this planet, we are temporarily and literally living in the enemy territory. It would be foolish to ignore that truth. I am not sure why we do. It is a basic teaching of the Bible. Jesus himself warns us about it multiple times. Paul and Peter both warn us and equip us against it. According to scripture, spiritual warfare is to be an expected and regular part of the Christian living experience. To paraphrase the quote at the beginning of this chapter, any friend of God's should expect to be an enemy of Satan.

Consider the fact that the very first thing that Jesus had to deal with after his baptism and fast was the temptations thrown at him by Satan in the wilderness. He was at the beginning of his recorded teaching ministry and immediately the devil tries to trip him up. What makes us think it would be any different for us? This is especially true in those times in which we are trying to kill our old man nature and turn to God for a deeper and more effective walk. It is in these times of recommitment and repentance that we should expect the spiritual warfare to be at its strongest. He wants to keep the old man relevant in your heart. As I have said in many a sermon, Satan cannot take you away from Jesus, but he can definitely discourage you, tempt you and try to ruin your testimony to others. Again, he tried it with Jesus. Should we expect any different?

There is an article in *The Christian Post* where actor Stephen Baldwin is interviewed. He comes from the famous Baldwin family in Hollywood and is a very outspoken evangelical Christian. Despite his family background, as often happens with outspoken Christian evangelical types, his openness on matters of faith has made him somewhat of a pariah in some Hollywood circles. Nevertheless, he speaks his mind. In the interview, he was asked how being a Christian has affected his acting career. Has it made it harder or easier? He answered the following:

"I definitely think that since I've become born again, if you understand in the supernatural realm the spiritual warfare that goes on every day, I've had far greater challenges on a personal level than before I became a Christian" (Stephen Baldwin).

He tells us right there something that every honest believer has found to be true. Becoming a Christian is not the end of all your problems. If anything, it might be the beginning of some. It invites spiritual warfare. We might not wish to admit this, but living in this world, it is easier to not be a Christian.

What? That's not a very evangelical approach to take. You are saying that my life would be easier if I don't become a Christian?

Well, maybe. Maybe not. But I do know this. Satan does not have to trouble the lives of those whom he already owns. He tends to leave them alone. This is perhaps the answer to the question that every pastor has been asked. Why do bad things happen to good people, while bad people seem to get away with murder? Well, it's the believers, specifically the dangerous believers that he is going to try to devour and discourage. A dangerous believer is any believer that is serious about their Christian life.

If you are tired of fighting that old man and struggling against the flesh, and you are committing yourself to move forward, which by the way is why I am assuming you are reading this book, then you are becoming a dangerous believer. You are dangerous to his plans. If there is any chance, someone else might see Jesus in you and the gospel message being promoted through you, then you are dangerous. Killing your old man is a red flag to your adversary. Expect resistance.

Psalm 143:12 speaks of the "adversary of our soul." But thankfully, it also speaks of God in his steadfast love cutting off the enemies of our soul. That is exactly what Jesus has done for us. That is the point of the new nature. That is the point of repentance. We are no longer obligated to live according to the old nature and, therefore, play into the hands of our enemy. We can resist.

James 4:7 says to "resist the Devil and he will flee from you." It is a verse that people love to quote and with good reason. It is a powerful promise tucked away in what some consider to be the most practical of all the New Testament letters. In those few words, we see where the real power lies. The real power is not us, but in us. Notice what James tells us there. We are to resist the devil. He doesn't say flee from the devil. He says resist him and he will flee from you! He is not scared of Rodney Peavy. But he is scared of he who indwells Rodney Peavy! So you see, in our spiritual battles, we actually have the advantage. That does not imply that our enemy is not to be feared. We cannot and should never underestimate him. But we do have the advantage.

Spiritual warfare is not what many people think, however. Many see it through the eyes of Hollywood. When they think of spiritual or demonic attacks, they visualize someone's head spinning or levitation or any other number of theatrical imaginings produced in movies and film over the years. It is for this reason I think many Christians do not take it seriously enough. Many see it is fiction or myth. It is, nonetheless, real though.

Real spiritual warfare is much more subtle than these Hollywood fantasies. While there can be supernatural happenings associated with spiritual warfare, I would argue that more times than not is much more unassuming than those images. It would be easy to classify those things as spiritual warfare. But what about feelings of shame and regret? That is not quite so noticeable, is it? In fact, we can explain those things in many different ways, not all of which are bad. Yet that is how our enemy operates. Again, just a little lie here and there will not draw our attention. A spinning head on a levitating little possessed girl, on the other hand, would raise suspicion!

Remember, in scripture, Satan is referred to as "the accuser of the brethren" in Revelation 12:10. Think about the significance of that name. He is referred to here by John as the one that accuses Christians. He is also called a deceiver. That is what he does.

This is important in those man-in-the-mirror moments when you are beating yourself up for once again falling into the same old sin. The thoughts you have that say you can't quit this or that God couldn't possibly love you, where do you think they come from?

Okay, but what if what he is saying about me is not a lie? What if I did mess up again? Well, if he is telling you the truth about yourself, he must be lying about how God relates to you as a result. Remember…he's the accuser of the brethren. There is nothing he would rather do than to have you doubt God's love and forgiveness.

Our enemy often does that by having us doubt God's word. This is why David tells us in Psalm 119 to hide God's word in our heart so that we may not sin against God (119:11). If we know God's word, then we know the truth. If we know the truth, then we won't fall for the lies our enemy would have us to believe about God's grace and mercy.

This has been his tactic since the Garden of Eden. He asked Eve if God really said not to eat of this tree? You will not die, he said. Even then, he was lying and leading them to doubt God's word, his truth. He may be powerful, but he is not that creative. Creation is God's nature. Satan's nature is destruction. And his tactics haven't really changed since that first sin in Eden. He uses the same tactic with us today.

Today, he might whisper in your ear and heart like this. Did God really say these things are sinful? Or again? God is getting tired of you. Can you really expect God to forgive you again? How could God love a screwup like you?

Sound familiar? To me, it does. I've heard it many times in those man-in-the-mirror moments. This is most likely spiritual warfare.

The enemy wants to discourage you and keep you from salvation or its benefits and from recommitting your life to a deeper more meaningful walk. He doesn't want you reckoning yourself alive to Christ. He wants nothing less than your destruction and mine. He wants to silence the gospel.

Granted, we have to be careful to not let the enemy have more credit than he deserves. We can't always just say "the devil made me do it." Sometimes it is just our old sinful nature. Sometimes we fall short completely on our own without any help from the enemy. In fact, I would say more times than not, this is the case. But the warfare is, nonetheless, real. Don't underestimate your enemy with some sort of self-deprecating claim of responsibility for everything bad that happens. That will lead to further shame and discouragement. At the same time, we cannot blame everything on him either.

The James 4:7 truth tells us that we can resist him. To choose instead to listen is just that, a choice. It is just like listening to the old man nature or the fleshy self. We choose to listen and obey or we choose to listen to and obey the Lord. Therein lies the battle. This is why we need help from beyond ourselves to engage in spiritual warfare.

Ephesians 6 gives us probably the most complete list of weaponry we have at our disposal in fighting the spiritual fight. It is here that Paul gives us the full armor of God teaching. Yet we cannot forget how he begins this teaching on spiritual warfare. He begins his teaching on this in verse 10, which says, "Finally, be strong in the Lord, and in the strength of his might." The strength is God's, not our own. For that matter, it is the armor of God, not the armor of Rod (or put your name here). I can't do it on my strength. Neither can you. Likewise, I cannot choose my new nature over my old, I cannot choose the Spirit over the flesh, and I cannot put the armor of God on without God's help.

We put on the belt of truth, breastplate of righteousness, sandals of gospel readiness, shield of faith, helmet of salvation, and the sword of the spirit. And we pray. You see, the defense strategy God gives us in Ephesians is completely dependent upon God's power. The only thing that really is ours in that list is the shield of faith, and that is our faith in him! So were really splitting hairs over whether it is ours or his. Regardless of how you look at it, the power to resist comes from the Lord.

Do not be surprised if you find yourself under attack! Trust me, I know the feeling. In my own experiences, I have seen an almost clockwork efficiency on the part of the enemy to attack me at the most predictable times. Just let me commit to improving some aspect of my spiritual life, and rest assured, I am soon going to be wrestling principalities and forces of evil and darkness.

The perfect example is this book. It has taken me much longer to finish it than I had originally planned because along the way, I have encountered every kind of distraction you can possibly imagine.

Every time I sit down to write, you can count on something happening to take my mind off of it. As much as I love writing, it makes for a real struggle. My prayer is that this means God has plans to use it for his good purposes, and Satan, my enemy, doesn't want anyone finding freedom from their sin after having read it and meditating on it. I wouldn't be surprised if many of you are not having a hard time finishing it, and not just because of my poor writing. The adversary of your soul doesn't want you to read the truth that is found here.

It is not just this book. Every time I am committing to any form of spiritual improvement, I can expect distractions, mental or emotional struggles, and even family issues. It is a little scary how easily I can predict it in my own life. But the predictability of it also helps me to prepare for it.

But if this is also you, be encouraged. This can only mean that the devil must be threatened by you. You are dangerous.

You may be thinking, *Yeah, but still it stinks. I don't want to fight. I don't want to wrestle.* Well, I agree. I don't want too either. But wrestling for a few decades on this Earth sure is better than wrestling for all eternity.

As believers, we are aliens and strangers on this Earth. As such, our wrestle free days are still ahead. Our spiritual warfare days will eventually come to an end. That is why those in Christ see death differently from the rest of the world. Those without faith are living the good life now, free of struggle and warfare. On the other hand, though the believer's time here may be one of struggle and fighting the flesh, the believer's good life time is coming. Their warfare free time may last for a few decades, a lifetime on this Earth. But our free time is without end.

Our enemy knows his time is limited too. He knows it. So don't expect him to go down without a fight. But using the shield of faith, belt of truth, and sword of the Spirit, know that the victory is ours. The adversary of your soul is beat already. He just doesn't know it, or perhaps he is such a liar that he has even come to lie to himself. Who knows? But be prepared to resist with all earnestness. Do not let the fear of attack keep you from enjoying the blessings that do come with wearing the armor of God.

Don't let his lies get to you. Dig in and resist. He loves to exploit the battle with our old man or flesh to his own advantage. Don't let him. Fight him with what you know to be true. Fight him with the truth of God's word and not with your emotions. Better yet, step aside and let God fight through you.

That is ultimately how we fight. We surrender to God.

That is ultimately how we win.

Fight. Fight. Fight.

And he will flee. Flee. Flee.

Looking Even Deeper

Personal/Group Discussion and Application

1. Read 1 Peter 5:6–11.

2. What five commands are we given in these verses to aid us in our withstanding the traps of the enemy?

3. What evidence have you seen of spiritual warfare both in your life and in the life of others?

4. Why do you think most believers do not take spiritual warfare seriously enough?

5. How can surrendering be part of our strategy in fighting our spiritual enemy?

6. Pray for God's help, wisdom, and strength to fight the enemy.

6

THE RECKONING

The Christian does not think God will love us because we are
good, but that God will make us good because He loves us.
—C. S. Lewis

Therefore we have been buried with him through baptism into
death, in order that as Christ was raised from the dead through
the glory of the Father, so we too might walk in newness of life.
—Romans 6:4

In the early chapters of this book, we have looked at the reality of our
sinful nature and the inevitability of having to wrestle with it. The
old man is a formidable adversary. So is our enemy the devil. Even
the best of us must deal with the fact that we are by nature sinners
and, therefore, weakened to sins power. This realization is a key step
in putting away the old nature; or as the old puritan writers put it,
mortifying the sinful nature or deeds of the flesh. To find the liberty
and peace promised to us in the life of faith, this realization is essen-
tial. If we truly long for this victory, if we want stop being held as a
spiritual hostage to our sinful selves, we must first know whom it is
we are fighting.

Of course, as we saw in the last chapter, we have an enemy that
is found outside ourselves. He is like a prowling lion seeking whom
he may devour. See 1 Peter 5:8. We just looked at this and more as

we meditated on the concept of spiritual warfare. But for now, let's again look within. Again, I am speaking of the old self or old nature, the old man we hope to finally put away.

As previously discussed, we are by nature broken. We are broken by the fall and the power of sin. This brokenness must be dealt with. It is inevitable. It cannot be ignored if we want to walk in the newness of life discussed in Romans 6:4. We should not be surprised by our tendency to sin nor should we just roll over and accept it. Too, we must not take God's grace for granted. Assuming that peace and liberty is what we truly want and that we now honestly see our old man nature for what it is, what do we do next? How do we ultimately put it to death?

Well, for our old man to be killed, we must be killed.

Whoa! Suicide? Is that what you're advocating. Some sort of spiritual suicide? No. Of course not. What I am advocating is a crucifixion.

In Romans 6:4, Paul speaks of being buried with Christ through baptism into death. He echoes this thought in Galatians 2:20, which says: "I have been crucified with Christ. It is no longer I who live, but Christ who lives in me. And the life I now live in the flesh I live by faith in the Son of God, who loved me and gave himself for me" (ESV).

The idea that we have been crucified when we come to faith in Christ is at the very heart of the struggle we are dealing with in this book. It is also at the very heart of the gospel message. After all, the ordinance of baptism is a symbolic representation of this crucifixion of our old sinful nature that has taken place in our hearts. However, it doesn't stop there. It also symbolizes a resurrection.

We are not just crucified with Christ. We are crucified so that we might be resurrected. And there can be no resurrection until there has first been a crucifixion. For a new life to begin, the old one must be dealt with.

Go back to Romans 6:4 again. Paul teaches us that this crucifixion has taken place so that we might be raised as Jesus was raised to walk in a newness of life. Put simply, to truly live, we first must die.

This is so important. If you get no further blessing from this writing than this truth, then let it be one that changes your life. Because it can. To truly live we first must die. God is not just trying to fix what is broken. He is trying to give us a new life altogether. To be new is much better than being a fixer-upper.

I learned this truth as I often do, the hard way, through a real-life lesson.

A few years back, I decided I needed a truck. After all, I was born and raised in the deep south and every good southern boy knows that every family needs a truck. How else can you haul things or move things that need moving, right? As a family man I needed one. I had been used to driving SUVs, mini vans, or family cars for a while, but I had driven a truck before and owned a few over the years. However, at this moment in my life, I didn't have one and felt like I needed one. So I began to look for one to meet my needs.

For budget's sake, I would be looking for a used vehicle. I finally found one that was in my price range…cheap. It looked good. According to the salesman, it operated well. I drove it and could find nothing really wrong with it other than a few cosmetic things and relatively high mileage. Of course, to this southern boy, cosmetic dings and scratches and high mileage were a sign that this had been a good, well-used, and dependable truck. These just meant it was a minor fixer-upper. As a bonus, it was inexpensive enough that my wife wouldn't leave me if I bought it! So I did just that. I bought it… as is.

Whenever you see "as is" on the window, you should pay close attention to what you are buying. I did. However, I was so excited about purchasing what was to me a "new" truck that I missed the significance of the "as is." I also missed many red flags that were warning me of a possible bad purchase. Instead, I just blindly signed the papers and drove away in my next life lesson.

I did not even make it home before the lesson would begin. The truck broke down literally on my way home from the dealership. I called them, only to be abruptly reminded that I had bought the truck "as is." So instead of basking in the joy of my first drive in a new vehicle, I instead had to have it towed on a weekend. This alone was expensive. Then I had to have a new alternator installed as well as a new battery. This, too, was not a cheap fix. But I had no choice.

But wait! It gets better. After driving it with a new alternator for at least a *whole* week (sarcasm intended), I began to hear a new knocking noise coming from the engine. I had a trusted mechanic look into the noise, only to discover that the engine had blown, just as I had suspected. To get this truck operational again, I would now have to have a completely new or at least a rebuilt engine installed. It would take weeks and would cost me more than I had originally paid for the truck in total.

As a matter of principle, I was determined to keep this truck. So I decided to fix it. Weeks and thousands of dollars later, it was operational again and had now cost me more than twice what it was worth. Even with the new engine, this truck would continue to break down and would in essence become a money pit. It was something all the time. Then as if that wasn't bad enough, within a year of having purchased it, the truck would be involved in an accident that would total it, or at least according to my insurance company, it was totaled. In reality, I had spent way more on this truck than I would ever receive from the insurance. I could have bought a new one, or at least put a substantial down payment on a new one for much less than I had spent on this fixer-upper truck, that I could no longer drive.

Lesson learned.

New is better than a fixer-upper.

This truth does not only apply to vehicle purchases. In fact, I guess there is probably room for some disagreement on the subject when it comes to car buying. But in spiritual matters, it is safe to say that being a new creation is better than being a fixer-upper.

The Bible teaches us that as Christians, we are new creations (2 Cor. 5:17). We have a new nature or a new self (Eph. 4:24). We are given a new heart (Ezek. 36:26). We are to walk in newness of life (Rom. 6:4). We are to be reborn (John 3:3). Do you sense a pattern? It would seem that God is not interested in fixing us as much as he is in making us new.

You see, just putting a new engine in that truck didn't change the fact that it was still an old lemon. It would never again run like a new one. It was a temporary fix to a lasting problem. I didn't need a new engine. I needed a new truck.

The same is true of our spiritual selves. We do not just need our problems fixed. We do not need our sinful nature fixed. What we need is a new nature! Like a rebuilt engine will never be the same as a brand-new one, a rebuilt or *fixed* nature is only putting off the inevitable. It doesn't need to be repaired. It needs to be made altogether new.

The good news is that this is exactly what has happened! By placing our faith in Jesus, by being born again, we have crucified the old nature and taken on a new one. We are no longer who we were before we come to Christ. We are new creations.

Of course, the first thought that we all probably have when thinking on this subject is the question "Why then do I still struggle with my old nature? Why do I still struggle with the same old sins?" Shouldn't being reborn take care of the struggle to follow the old nature? At first glance, perhaps. But reality teaches us differently.

The reason the struggle is still there is because the old nature still exists. It has not yet been destroyed. It still exists. However, the "us" that was obligated to follow the old nature has been crucified so that we could now live resurrected and beholden to our new nature. The old nature is still there; it is just dead to us and we are dead to it in the sense that it no longer has any power over us except that which we allow it to have. We are reborn with a new nature. That is who we are now. Even on those trying days when we may not feel like it, I am now who Christ says I am.

You may be thinking that this is just wordplay. It is not. Go back to Paul's rant in Romans 7. He recognized in verse 21 of that chapter a law or principle at work within the heart of every believer that states that evil or that old fallen nature is always there with him causing him to do things that the new Paul doesn't want to do. The same is true for you and me. That is why we must not only believe this law or principle of the presence of our sinful selves to be true, but we must also believe with our whole heart that this sinful self is not who we are anymore. We may occasionally listen to it and do what it says, but it is not my identity. It is dead to us. We don't have to do what it says anymore. With the help of the Holy Spirit which now indwells us, we can instead choose to follow the inclinations of our new nature.

Romans 6:11 in the King James Version reads, "Likewise reckon ye also yourselves to be dead indeed unto sin, but alive unto God through Jesus Christ our Lord." This is a significant and possibly paradigm shifting verse.

The word *reckon* there is often translated *consider* in more modern translations. That, of course, is an accurate rendering. However, I prefer the word *reckon*, and not just because it reminds me of my southern slang upbringing and manner of speech, which it does; but I like it because it more accurately paints a picture of what this considering is to truly be. *Reckoning*, in this sense, is the same terminology that we might use in accounting or bookkeeping.

For the books to reckon or reconcile, the figures much all must match up. To reckon the figures is to acknowledge the truth. To be true, what we say we have on the books must match up with what we actually have on hand. That is what Paul is telling us to do. By reckoning ourselves dead to sin, we are acknowledging the truth. We are accounting for the truth. What we say we have, a new nature, must match up to what we do just as what we say we are no longer must match up to what we no longer do.

We are dead to sin. It no longer has any power over us. It is still powerful, but not as powerful as the new nature to which we now follow. Sin is not dead to us. It still exists. We are instead dead to sin. To reckon ourselves dead to it is to choose new life over death. It is to choose the new nature over the old. The new is what we are now. It is a choice we have been given as part of our free will. We can now choose to not listen to the old nature. But we first must reckon ourselves dead to it. That doesn't mean the old nature is no longer a powerful influence. It most certainly is. That is why we have the struggle with repeated and besetting sins. That is also why we are commanded to reckon and do it daily.

It is also dangerous to underestimate the influence of the old nature. Forgive me for being graphic, but you cannot keep a dead corpse in the room for very long before it begins to be an influence.

Even though it is powerless, if it is not dealt with, it will soon begin to stink up the room. But it only has power over you because you have chosen to keep it in the room. Now being indwelled by Christ, you can put it out.

Again, I think this is why Jesus tells us to take up our cross *daily* (Luke 9:23). We must reckon ourselves dead to the old self *daily*. God has given us the new resurrected nature. We must decide which one we are going to follow. The giving of the new nature happens once upon accepting Jesus as our Lord and Savior and last for all our lives. But the reckoning ourselves dead to the old we must do again and again until that day when we finally have victory over it for all eternity. It is part of the lifelong process we call sanctification.

To reckon ourselves dead to sin means we believe with all our heart that that old sinful nature is no longer who we are. It means believing this so deeply that we choose to instead follow the new nature. Will we still stumble from time to time? Yes. See the previous chapters. But the truth of the matter is that we no longer have too.

This is why it is so much better to be made new versus just being fixed. So many in our day look at Christianity as simply an attempt at being better people. They look at faith as an attempt be improved. I guess those who follow this interpretation mean well. It is not a bad thing to want to be a better person. But I think this explanation only serves to discourage and frustrate those of us who live in the real world. It frustrates because try as hard as you wish, you are still going to fall short of both God's holiness and even your own expectations. We then begin to see ourselves primarily through the lens of our successes and failures. More often failures. And the truth is that we are probably even worse than we think.

This is why it is so liberating to see ourselves instead in the light of Christ. Through him and to him, we have been reconciled because we are no longer who we once were. God is not interested is just fixing you. He wants to give you a new life and wants you walk in that newness of life and wants to share that new life experience with you. He wants to help you walk in that newness. In fact, go back to Galatians 2:20, and you will see that it is Jesus that empowers us to walk in this newness of life. We cannot do it on our own strength.

This relationship with him is what makes it possible. It is what he wants for you. He wants you to know that he loves you too much to just accept you as a fixer-upper. He wants more for you than that. Not because you deserve it, but because he wants it for you. He wants to give you a new life and he has, through the cross and resurrection.

But we must also remember, it is not enough to simply consider ourselves dead to sin. We must also consider ourselves alive in and unto Christ. That means looking to him for strength, wisdom, guidance, help, assurance, and peace. It means denying self and committing ourselves to Christ likeness. It means daily communion through prayer, worship, and Bible study. It means singlemindedness in all our endeavors. You see, it is in him that we find what is lacking in our old man nature. It cannot be found in our selves or in any other place. It is in him that we reckon our true identity.

Is it time for a reckoning in your life?

Yes. It's time to reckon yourselves dead to sin and alive in Christ.

No matter your performance or mine, this new nature is now who we are. We need to acknowledge it. No matter how many times I find myself discouraged by my faults, I am a born-again believer. A reckoning has taken place in my heart. I know the truth of who I am no matter what you think, what others think, what my enemy thinks and no matter what my old man self thinks.

According to God's truth, this is who I am. I am a new creation. So are you!

Ask me if I really believe this to be true.

My answer which comes from a lifetime of stumbling and getting back up again is simple and emphatic… I reckon so.

Looking Even Deeper

Personal/Group Discussion and Application

1. Read Galatians 2:19–21.

2. What is meant by verse 20 where it says, "The life which I now live in the flesh I live by faith in the Son of God"?

3. What is meant by verse 21? What does it teach us about our struggle with the old man nature?

4. In your own words, what does it mean to "reckon" yourself dead to sin?

5. Do you find this reckoning difficult or easy? Why?

6. Pray and ask God to help you reckon yourself dead to sin and alive in Christ.

7

THE TURNING

Repentance is the vomit of the soul.
—Thomas Brooks

The difference between true and false repentance lies in this:
the man who truly repents cries out against his heart; but
the other, as Eve, against the serpent, or something else.
—John Bunyan

All the longer your delay, the more your sin gets
strength and rooting. If you cannot bend a twig, how
will you be able to bend it when it is a tree?
—Richard Baxter

Repent therefore, and turn again, that your sins may be blotted out.
—Acts 3:19

This reckoning we have been looking at includes more than just the recognition of the need to change. That is the easy part. If it is a real reckoning, it requires action. To reckon oneself dead to sin, we must also reckon ourselves alive in Christ. We have a word for this redirective reckoning. It is called repentance.

Most all believers have heard at one point or another along their journey of faith a definition of repentance. They probably heard it from a pastor or preacher or in something they have read along the way. That definition probably went something like this. Repentance is to turn around, to go in a different direction. It is to turn from your sin and go in opposite direction. It is a spiritual u turn. Well, those definitions are accurate to a degree. Repentance is turning away from your sin. But it is also much more than that. It is also perhaps the most powerful tool we have in fighting the fight against the nature of the old man.

It might be easier to discuss what repentance is not. Repentance is not only turning away from sin. It is also simultaneously turning to God. Hence, the reckoning ourselves dead to one and then alive in the other. It is not enough to just quit something. Quitting can be done on our own strength…at least for a while. It usually doesn't last. That is the danger of weak or false repentance. We usually try to do it by our own strength instead of depending on the Holy Spirit for help. And guess what inevitably happens? We usually wind up right where we started, back in front of that mirror of despair and self-loathing. True repentance means taking our eyes off our sinful self and fixing our eyes on the One that is able to actually remove our sins from us, Jesus.

Repentance is also not simply feeling guilty. It is not feeling bad over something we have done. It is not that sick feeling we get in the pit of our stomach when we realize we have messed up. Even the vilest of sinners, the most desperate nonbeliever out there can experience feelings of remorse and shame over their transgressions. More times than not, this feeling of regret is usually mixed with the realization of the pending negative consequences we may be facing. Put simply, it is possible that our feelings are simply a dread of the coming storm we have created with our actions or fear of getting caught if we have not yet been found out. If we had not been caught in our sin, we might not even feel this sense of regret or shame. So let's not confuse fear and regret with repentance. True repentance is so much more than these emotions and is not meant to be an emotional weight or a burden as regret and shame often are. On the contrary, repentance is liberating.

Repentance is also not apologizing. Again, anyone can apologize. That doesn't make it sincere, and it doesn't constitute a turning away from sin. It is possible to apologize and then go right back to the behavior for which we have apologized. In this instance, it is easy to see that true repentance has not taken place.

I remember once a situation in my own life where someone hurt me with their words and actions. Something was taken out of context that I had said and done in a church council meeting, and it was retold in such a way as to make me look bad. Thankfully, I had witnesses to back up my version of the incident, and I didn't have to say anything to the person. Others confronted them for me. An apology was offered to me, and I accepted. Nevertheless, the damage was done. After a few more weeks, I was still having to deal with the gossip surrounding the accusation. And it once again came to my attention that things were still begin said by the original accuser. I confronted them on what was still being said and their response to me was "I've already apologized. What else do you want from me?" What else indeed. I wanted them to stop lying about me! It was obvious the original apology meant nothing. It was meaningless and was definitely not repentance.

How often do we do that with God? We say "I am sorry" and think that fixes everything. The sad part is that unlike me and above-mentioned person, God knows when I say it whether or not I really mean it.

Our "apologies" are usually the instinctive response to getting caught. Even if the regretful feelings are genuine, it is not repentance if in our heart we have no intention on stopping. That is the danger of sin and why it should never be played with or underestimated. More times than not, it feels good. It is fun. We like it. This aspect of the sinful nature makes it even harder to repent. It is difficult to repent of something that you enjoyed, especially when you know in your heart that if you had the opportunity again, you would probably take it. This is how so many people, and yes, so many believers fall into addictions and besetting sins. It is a truly a trap. And we are not speaking of just things like drugs and sex. It can be something as seemingly benign as telling or listening to a dirty joke or engaging in gossip. Let's be honest. Those things can be fun too. But it is still a trap meant to keep you from true repentance. Put simply, apologies while good, are just fluff if they don't lead to a change.

True repentance is not only feeling sorry for your actions or saying you are sorry for your actions but agreeing deep down in your heart with God that they are sinful. Repentance is a heartfelt agreement with your creator that a change needs to take place, so much so that you are looking to him for help in making that change. Again, it is turning from your sin and turning toward God in full agreement of the need to do so.

Let's consider for a moment one of the greatest stories of repentance we have in the scriptures. It is the repentance of King David. David was guilty of some of the worst sins. I, of course, am speaking of his infamous sin with Bathsheba. He was prideful, he lusted, he committed adultery, and then conspired to commit a murder in an effort to cover up his sin. Let's face it. David was rotten. Yet he is still seen as Israel's greatest king and a man after God's own heart. How can that be? Well, it is because he repented.

Repentance works the same for you and me. It can take a dirty ugly sinner and turn them into a man or woman after God's own heart. As bad as David had messed up, that segment of his life is not for what he is primarily remembered. Sure, we remember it. But it does not define David. It is merely a chapter in a greater story. We see the story changer of David's repentance in Psalm 51 and Psalm 32.

Once David was confronted by Nathan the prophet about his sin and subsequent cover-up, he repented. He then wrote Psalm 51 and 32. These two psalms are two of my favorites. This is probably due to the fact that even though we know the occasion for which they were written, they are still so general in nature that the principles included could apply to my sin and your sin just as easily. While they are general in application, their targets are sighted directly on the human heart's response to Holy Spirit conviction.

True repentance is the response to true Holy Spirit conviction. To experience Holy Spirit conviction, we must first be indwelled by the Holy Spirit. All believers are indwelled by the Holy Spirit upon belief. However, we must also be open to the Spirit's leading. This happens when we reckon ourselves dead to sin and alive to Christ. This is what happens when we regularly surrender to the Holy Spirit. Then we can feel more than just regret over getting caught. It is then we can agree with God and act accordingly.

When you look at Psalm 51, we see David still in the midst of his repentance. Notice the honesty of this psalm. David makes no excuses. He doesn't even pull "the devil made me do it" excuse out. He also doesn't blame it on Bathsheba. He doesn't say, "It was her fault. She shouldn't have been bathing on her rooftop in plain view of the palace. Besides, I didn't force her." Instead, he takes full responsibility for his actions. He even says in verse 4 that God is justified in his anger with him. This is David's agreeing with God.

He also recognizes in 51:4 that his sin was against God. Granted, he sinned against Bathsheba and, most assuredly, against her husband Uriah. He also sinned against the people of his kingdom and against his advisors. But ultimately, the sin was first and foremost against God himself. It was God after all that transformed David from a young shepherd boy into the greatest king Israel would ever know. By hurting these other people, David sinned against God, who put him in his position of leadership. I do not believe David was saying that he had not sinned against anyone else so much as he was just saying that the greatest sin was against God. Ultimately, being God's man made this sin an affront to God himself. The same is true of you and I today. We are his children. When we sin, we sin against God our Father.

Psalm 32 was written much later, after his repentance had seen its fruit. It is similar to the first prayer song in Psalm 51; in that, David was brutally honest and owned his mistakes. But in Psalm 32, he speaks from the perspective of looking back on this dark period of his life and seeing how much better off he is now in comparison to how he was then. Many consider 32 a sequel to 51. Looking back, he speaks of the danger of keeping his sin bottled within his own heart. He describes the emotions with which he was wrestling prior to repentance. Like Paul in Romans 7, David was having his own man-in-the-mirror moment. He was stressed and depressed to point that his physical body was suffering. You see, the spiritual has a way of bleeding over into our physical selves. It cannot be ignored. Our spiritual self is just as much who we are or perhaps even more so than our physical, and so the two cannot be separated. David felt as if he was being crushed (Ps. 32:3–4). That is a great description of the Christian resisting repentance. By refusing to repent, we are inviting this crushing. Don't be surprised if this crushing makes you physically ill.

In both of these beautiful psalms, David uses the same three words to name his sin. He uses the word *sin, iniquity*, and transgression. This is not by coincidence. I believe it to be intentional. Each word implies a different understanding of sin. David didn't seem to want to leave any sin uncovered in his act of repentance and in his following songs and prayers. I think God inspired him to do so for our benefit.

The word *sin* is more general than the other two. It implies "missing the mark" or a "falling short." It is anything that falls outside the will of God. It is doing wrong. It is not doing right. It doesn't necessarily convey in its meaning intent or desire. It is simply what happens when we give in to that old man nature. A simple sin might include sins of commission and sins of omission. They may or may not be intentional. They are, nevertheless, against the will of God.

The word *transgression*, on the other hand, implies something different. It takes it a little bit deeper. A transgression is sin that is committed intentionally. It is the conscious choice to do something of which we know God will not be pleased. It is willingly choosing our own will over God's. It is knowing right and wrong and ultimately choosing wrong. It is often those sins committed in the heat of the moment that we know to be inappropriate, yet we still choose to carry it through.

Iniquity takes sinfulness even a step further than the word transgression. To commit an iniquity is to commit a premeditated sin. What David did when he saw Bathsheba on that roof was a transgression. When he had Uriah sent to the front to be killed to cover up his sin with Bathsheba, that was an iniquity. It is a planned continuance in a sin.

Needless to say, David had all the bases covered with these three categories. Whatever besetting sin with which your old self keeps dragging you to that mirror of regret, it is safe to say that it falls into one these three-word descriptions. It is of these that David is encouraging us to repent. David should know. But David is not alone.

The very first recorded message we have Jesus preaching is one of repentance. It says in Matthew 4:17 that Jesus's very first public teaching was "Repent, for the kingdom of heaven is at hand." Likewise, the message of repentance is all throughout the New Testament letters. This turning away from our sin and turning toward God is the key to killing our old man.

David touched on this in Psalm 51:10 when he asked God to create in him a clean heart and to renew a steadfast or right spirit within him. You see, David knew that the repentance was his to do, but the changing was God's to do. He didn't ask God to help him change. He asked God to do the changing…or more specifically, the recreating.

Repentance isn't about doing better. It's about looking to the right source for direction and guidance and help. The result is that we will do better with his help.

Repentance is also not something we do once. With every sin comes the opportunity to repent. It is a continual thing we do. One of those unknown Puritan writers from *The Valley of Vision* I love to read wrote once "I repent of my repentance, I need my tears to be washed." He was simply expressing his emotions over his need to sometimes repent more than once for the same sin. The whole premise of this book is that sometimes we have to come back to the same old sin. It doesn't mean that we haven't truly repented. We can honestly repent and then later slip back into a familiar sin. It happens.

Practically speaking, when this happens, there is really no point in debating within our hearts whether or not we really repented or not in our previous outcries. Whether we did or not, the point is that we now need too again. That's okay. If we didn't originally, well then, we need to now. And if we did, we need to again. And the fact that you are under conviction on the subject means that God is giving you the opportunity to do just that. God has made provision for you through repentance. Don't miss the blessing he is offering you through repentance by putting it off until a later time, to a time when you think you will know for sure that you really mean it. Do it now. Turn away from it and turn toward God. Don't wait for the heavy hand of God to crush you as David did. Embrace the immediate gift that is repentance.

I've often heard repentance described as starting over. I appreciate the sentiment and, I am sure that I have described it in that manner myself somewhere down the line. However, I don't think that is accurate either. It is not starting over. Starting over implies will power on my part to correct things. That is not repentance. Repentance is trusting in and believing the promises of God. It is putting that belief into an act of absolute trust and surrender. It is part of the everyday experience of the believer. Starting over also implies that we have lost ground and are back at the very beginning of our faith. That is not accurate either. Messing up along the way doesn't mean I am starting over as a new believer. Repentance is an instrument that every believer can use to keep going in the right direction. If you are truly repenting, then you are going and growing in the right direction. It is a weapon, the most powerful weapon we have against the old man. It is not going back to the beginning. It is changing the forward momentum of our Christian walk. It is choosing the new creation nature over the old man nature. Learn from the experience and repent.

Weep. Mourn. Cry over your sin. Agree with God over your sin. Turn from your sin. And then most importantly, turn to God. That is repentance.

If it happens again, repeat.

Continue in the turning.

Looking Even Deeper

Personal/Group Discussion and Application

1. Read 2 Corinthians 7:9–10.

2. What do you think is the difference between sorrow according to the will of God or godly sorrow and the sorrow that the world produces? What is the usual outcome of each?

3. In your own words, what is your own definition of repentance?

4. Knowing the background, how does Psalm 51 make you feel when you read it?

5. Have you ever felt like David in Psalm 51 and 32?

6. Think of a time when you repented. How did it affect you?

7. Pray and ask God to show you the need for repentance and the strength to do so.

8

THE LEDGE

You should not believe your conscience and your feelings more than
the Word which the Lord who receives sinner preaches to you.

—Martin Luther

Whoever trusts in his own mind is a fool, but he
who walks in wisdom will be delivered.

—Proverbs 28:26

It is unreliable at best. The human heart and all of its accompanying
emotions are part of who we are, yet we must be honest about it. Can
our feelings be trusted? It has been my experience that they cannot.
Feelings are fickle.

Feelings come and go. In a matter of minutes, our minds can
experience both calm and peace and then grow into anger and frustration. These same feelings can last for years or can change in an
instant, for all too often, they depend upon circumstances. Those
circumstances can be something as minor as what we had for lunch
or a change in the weather or something as serious as a major life
change or even the death of a loved one. They can be overwhelming
and even crippling and seemingly impossible to move beyond and at
the same time be as fleeting and unpredictable as the wind. Feelings
can be harmless, and they can be destructive. They keep life interesting to say the least.

You can see just how destructive it can be to follow our feelings by looking around in the modern-day culture. The new trend in our day is to follow your feelings even if it means to disregard the facts. If we feel a certain way, then it can't be wrong and must be true. Things we have taken for granted for millennia as being accepted fact are now being seen as social constructs and relative truths and, therefore, subject to change as our emotions change. It can be something as basic as gender or race. The result of these feelings-based philosophies is higher than ever suicide rates, divorces, broken families, and ever-increasing mental disorder diagnoses. You see, when we follow our feelings, the end result is that there is my truth and there is your truth and nothing really can be trusted or depended upon with certainty. If anything can be true, then those things that hurt us aren't right or wrong and there is no hope of overcoming. The result of this relativistic philosophy is chaos. And we get lost. Hope is lost and uncertainty rules the day. This is true politically, morally, and spiritually. It begins when we let feelings take priority over truth. This approach fits right into our enemy's playbook.

This is not to say that our feelings are inherently evil or that they aren't important. Emotions are part of who we are as being made in the image of God. In scripture, we see God angry, grieved, joyful, happy, and moved to act and even change his mind. God has emotions. And by his creative wisdom, so do we. Our feelings and those of others are real and should matter to us; in that, our creator saw fit to instill this part of his nature into each of us.

After all, emotions can lead us to do great things. They lead us to show compassion and empathy toward others. They inspire us to share with others and to exhibit selfless acts of mercy.

Feelings can also lead us to do some extremely selfish things as well. Emotions can cause us to have outbursts of anger, rage, and violence and can frequently lead us to make some impulsive and life altering poor choices. How often do we read or hear in the news of someone's life being ruined over a reaction to what is later seen as the most trivial of issues? A food order that was wrong or being cut off in traffic are poor reasons to ruin a life, yet it happens. Just this week, there was an incident reported in the local news in which a man was killed over an argument over a bowling ball. A man was killed because he used someone else's bowling ball by mistake. A life was ended and a family lost a father, husband, son, and brother over a bowling ball. A trivial reason for lives to be ruined. And it all happened because of unchecked emotions.

Unfortunately, while hopefully not to that extreme, how we feel at the moment is often our first and most powerful driving motivation in life. The problem with this is that how I feel right now might not be how I feel later. And how I feel is often not based upon reality and definitely not often based upon motives of godliness. To trust our momentary emotions might lead us to a later regret.

But the problem of emotions is more than just losing our temper or acting rashly in the heat of the moment. For the maturing believer, grasping the uncertainty of our feelings is especially important when it comes to our overcoming our old man nature. To kill our old man, we must be able to distinguish between the emotions of the moment and the truth of God's promises. Otherwise, we become caught in the trap of our own everchanging emotional mind and play right into hands of our old man nature and the hands of our enemy. We can get caught up in the feelings of failure and shame and fail to move beyond them. We can become spiritually stagnant.

How is it that our own heart can't be trusted? After all, shouldn't our own heart only want what is best for us? Shouldn't we be able to trust it above all other advisers, if for no other reason than that of self-preservation? We should be, except for one little and inescapable fact. We live in a fallen world and have a fallen nature. We are sinners. As a result, out heart can't be trusted to always lead us in the right path.

Jeremiah touched on this in his prophecy. In Jeremiah 17:9, it says, "The heart is deceitful above all things, and desperately sick; who can understand it?" Desperately sick, he says. Sounds familiar, doesn't it? It is basically the same sentiment of Paul in that Romans 7 man-in-the-mirror moment. He knew his heart couldn't be trusted to always do what it should, and that evil was always right there with him. If it is true of our hearts ability to make proper choices, shouldn't it also be true concerning our own feelings? The heart is deceitful. In other words, it sometimes lies to us. Our feelings aren't always, but most certainly can be based upon lies.

I have seen firsthand the reality of this truth. My feelings can't always be trusted, especially in specific areas of my life. My wife and I have a couple of expressions we use in times of emotional distress. I should say they are my expressions. They are panic phrases I often say to her when I find myself in a situation where my emotions are overwhelming me. These phrases probably don't make a lot of sense outside of our family walls, but they are precious to me. Because sometimes I can be emotional, as can we all. In fact, sometimes I can get so caught up in my feelings that I can't judge reasonably. Not always, but it happens. The older I get, the better able I am to recognize when this emotional phenomenon is happening. When I sense I am slipping into a state of emotional distress, I sometimes turn to my wife for help. I'll ask her to "talk me off the ledge" or else "I need you to keep me from going down the rabbit hole." These silly expressions are my way of asking for her help. I'm asking her to inject some truth and reason into the situation; in that, my feelings are making it near impossible to act with wisdom. In those emotional moments, I can often only see the worst-case scenario being played out and am often blind to how God is, nonetheless, working in the situation. My emotions can easily rob me of hope. In those moments, my emotions are winning.

I am thankful that God has given me a wife that can steady me when my feelings are making me unsteady. She is truly a gift from God. I am amazed at the ease at which she can rein in my emotional landslides. She does it by basically following my pleas for assistance with simple and loving reminders of some simple truths in the situation, whatever it might be. These are truths that I am having a hard time remembering at the moment because I am so blinded by my feelings. This truth almost always differs with how I am feeling in those moments and often come upon me like a slap in the face. These simple declarations of truth in turn brings me back down to a frame of mind in which I can discern between reality and emotional turmoil. Truth is the solution to the lack of trustworthiness exhibited by our feelings. It lifts the cloudiness created by our storm of emotions.

This isn't only true for me in those emotional moments. It is true for all of us. This is especially important when we are engaging our flesh or self or our spiritual enemy. The greatest temptation we might face in those moments is to trust how we feel. Emotions often get strong when we are facing spiritual battles. It is natural.

As a pastor, I have had countless counsel sessions with people who stated something along these lines. "But I just don't feel very Christian." Or "I don't feel as if I am saved." Or "I don't feel as if God has forgiven me." They are discouraged because they don't *feel* as if they are experiencing any spiritual growth or victories. The problem is not their reality. It is their feelings. You see, the whole reason they had come to me for counsel in the first place was because they were trying to overcome some spiritual obstacle that they were up against and had a genuine desire to overcome. They were under conviction. This is a good thing!

Spiritually stagnated believers don't have that desire to move forward or overcome and lost people don't experience Holy Spirit conviction. Only those indwelled by the Holy Spirit would be engaged in such an internal battle. I've never had a lost person come to me and complain that they don't feel like a Christian! So while these feelings themselves may be real and should be taken into consideration to some degree, they do not change the reality of our spiritual standing before God. Thus, they do not need to be the determining factor in our actions moving forward.

It is in these moments that we must remember that feelings aren't reality. I can feel like I am not a born-again believer in the heat of the moment. It's probably because I am not acting like one in that moment. But that doesn't change the fact that God has saved me from my sins and given me eternal life and made me a new creation, which nothing, including my own shortcomings can take away from me! If anything, for the believer, this feeling of inadequacy might just be the proof that I am a believer! After all, if I wasn't a follower of Christ, would I really care that I didn't feel like a Christian? Remember, one of Satan's nicknames is the "accuser of the brethren." It makes his work so much easier when we choose to trust our feelings over the truth of God's word.

The point I am trying to make is simple actually. Truth trumps feelings every time.

The next time you feel as if you are still a slave to the old man nature, remember the truth of God's word in Romans 6:6, which says that this old nature has been crucified and you are no longer a slave to sin. The next time you stumble and follow the old-man nature and feel as if there is no way God could possibly forgive you *again* for same old sin, remember Romans 8:1, which says, "There is therefore now no condemnation to them which are in Christ Jesus." Let God's Holy Spirit bring to remembrance the truth of God's word. Let the Holy Spirit talk you off the ledge of emotional distress. Then after acknowledging the truth, act accordingly. Each time you choose truth over feelings, the old man nature is weakened.

Again, feelings in and of themselves are not good or bad. They are what they are. But don't let how you feel rob you of the joy that comes from the assurance of salvation and the promise of God's love and grace.

This next sentence is not a popular message, but it is the truth. You are going to fail from time to time! I do. We all do. God knows you are going to fail. We shouldn't be content in that knowledge, but it also shouldn't surprise us. It is not the end of your spiritual growth. It is simply part of it. Because when it happens, God has made a way for you to get up and try again. It is repentance. It is grace. It is forgiveness. When we accept that, we grow. We move forward. Don't let your feelings hide that reality from you!

One way to combat this tendency is to be so familiar with the truth of God's word, his precious promises, that no feeling either positive or negative will ever be able to convince you of anything outside of God's word and will. One thing I do to help with this is to always keep a copy of God's word within arm's reach, in the event that I find myself alone and slipping down the hole of emotional uncertainty. The psalms are filled with reassuring truths for such moments. Also, turn to your spouse or find a friend you can trust to give you reminders of the truth in those emotional moments. Again, my wife has talked me off the ledge of emotional distress more times than I can count. It works. These are important steps in combatting that old man nature.

First John 3:20 is a great verse and one that you should hang on your wall or tape to the dashboard of your car or put in some other prominent daily significant place. It is one that you need to read regularly and live daily. It says, "Beloved, if our heart condemns us, God is greater than our heart, and knoweth all things." Isn't that a truth worth remembering? It is a life-altering truth. It acknowledges that our heart might from time to time condemn us, but most importantly, it reminds us that God is greater than our heart. Which one are you going to trust the next time you are doubting your relationship with the Lord? Your feelings or God's truth?

Don't ignore conviction, but don't trust your feelings. Again, and put as simply as I can, our feelings aren't facts. They aren't necessarily our reality. What God has done for us and is still doing in each of us is greater than our old fickle and deceitful heart! That is our reality. He is our reality.

How I feel right now can't change who God is and what he has done for me! How I feel at the moment will most likely pass, but God's promises are everlasting. So step off the deceitful emotional ledge and trust in the promises of God.

Looking Even Deeper

Personal/Group Discussion and Application

1. Read Romans 8:1.

2. How does the truth of this verse line up with your current feelings?

3. Do you agree with the author's sentiment that feelings aren't facts? Why or why not?

4. Has there ever been a time when your feelings led you astray? Have you ever felt that you were not saved because of your sin?

5. Do you ever get caught up in your emotions? What steps can you take to "talk yourself off the ledge" of emotional distress?

6. What does 1 John 3:20 mean to you?

7. Pray that God will help you understand your feelings and to know the truth of his love for you.

9

Knock. Breathe. Shine.

No matter how dear you are to God, if pride is harboured in
your spirit, He will whip it out of you. They that go up in their
own estimation must come down again by His discipline.
—Charles Spurgeon

Because the Lord disciplines the one he loves, and
he chastens everyone he accepts as his son.
—Hebrews 12:6 (NIV)

In our quest to evict our old man nature, the greatest mistake we
can make is to think it is something that can be accomplished by
our own strength. We need a strength that is beyond our own. This
diabolical old man will not leave willingly or easily. We can't just talk
him away or wish him away. We can't even work him out of our lives
with good intentions and righteous deeds. With all our efforts, we
must know that he can still kick, he can still scream and he can still
bite. And as we have looked at in previous chapters, just when you
think you have pushed him out, suddenly he can reappear, and you
find yourself fighting the same battle all over again. And even if we
understand that we need God to do the housecleaning for us, the
one thing we don't really want to face is that sometimes this God
led eviction comes with a price. Sometimes, the method God uses to
evict the old man is discipline.

Discipline never comes easy. If it were to come easy, it would lose its effectiveness and, therefore, would cease to be discipline. This is especially true when it is God that is carrying out the discipline. Simply knowing that we need to act differently is not always enough. Sometimes even knowing God's will in particular situations is not enough to alter our behaviors. Many times we know what to do but aren't motivated enough to do it. In those instances, we might just inadvertently force God to use to the method of discipline to set us on a straight path. Knowing the truth and knowing his will, we stubbornly still often choose to follow the old man instead of living as a new creation. Put simply, God must often take extra steps to get our attention and to help us break free from the cycle of sin, shame, and repetition. That extra step is discipline.

The idea of God disciplining his children is not a popular subject, and there aren't as many modern sermons or writings on the subject as there probably should be, especially considering how it is such a vital part of personal spiritual growth. Perhaps it is because we often confuse discipline with punishment and, therefore, have a hard time associating it with a God who loves unconditionally. But the reconciling of these thoughts requires us to remember that discipline is not punishment. Not at all.

Punishment implies a revenge of sorts, being forced upon us as a result of our shortcomings. It usually is thought of as coming from someone who only wants to hurt us and bring us down, not to help us and lift us up. Punishment is usually a response made in anger and often has selfish motives. We can learn from punishment, but we don't usually grow from it. In fact, if we learn anything from punishment it is usually to hate or despise and to put ourselves first in the future. It can even teach us to become more creative in regard to our future sins and our feeble attempts to cover them so that we might avoid more punishment. You see, punishment can make us even more determined to sin, not less. Punishment in this sense does not draw us closer to God. It would probably do just the opposite and create a resentment and distance between us and our Lord. This is why God does not punish his children. He disciplines them.

Now this does not mean that God does not punish sin. He is a holy and righteous God that cannot tolerate sin. But the good news of the gospel is that our punishment, the punishment we most certainly deserve was put on Jesus, not on us. Again, it is the pain of grace. Isaiah 53:5 says, "He was pierced through for our transgressions, He was crushed for our iniquities, The chastening for our well being fell upon Him, And by His scourging we are healed." The cross was our punishment. The penalty or punishment for my sins has already been administered.

This is something we often forget and something our enemy definitely wants us to forget. God is not sitting on some throne keeping tally marks of every time I stumble so that he can punish me for them once again. If that were the case, every day would be another day of being taken to the spiritual woodshed. God has already delivered the punishment for my sins, once and for all (Rom. 6:10; 1 Pet. 3:18; 1 John 2:2). This punishment fell upon the back of my Savior. It resulted in his crucifixion. It is the only means by which a sinner such as I can now have a relationship with a righteous and holy God. His holiness has been satisfied and remains uncompromised, and my sins have been punished. There is now nothing standing between us. He is not, therefore, going to punish me again for sins already paid for by Jesus, the perfect sacrifice. Since punishment has already been delivered, I can now approach him as my heavenly Father and have a real and personal relationship free of the fear of punishment. But coming with a relationship with a holy and righteous God, must be the acceptance that God loves us too much to just leave us stuck in our repetitious cycles of sin and shame. Because fellowship between us with our sinful nature and him with his loving nature, he must still discipline us when we stray.

Discipline, however, has the opposite cause and effect as that of punishment. Discipline as we are speaking of here is a product of love and devotion, not one of revenge or selfishness or as would be in the case of God's punishment, the result of a holy demand for justice or righteousness. Parents do not discipline their children to penalize them or because they dislike them or because they expect perfection from them. They do it because they love them and they want them to learn self-control and respect, qualities that will help them live productive and meaningful lives. In fact, some would argue that to not discipline your children is a form of abuse; in that, you are not preparing your inexperienced children to deal with all the complexities of the life that naturally and inevitably will come as they grow older and when living among other individuals. Genuine discipline is necessary for growth, and it always comes from someone that genuinely cares about our well-being and future. Punishment is payment. Discipline teaches.

Now, if this is true of our earthly parents and relationships, shouldn't it also be true of our heavenly Father? Of course it is. It is no wonder that there are several scriptures which teach us that we shouldn't think it unusual or be discouraged by God's discipline when it occurs. Some examples can be found in Deuteronomy 8:5–6, Job 5:17, Hebrews 12:5–11, and many others. The book of Proverbs is filled with passages on the discipline which comes from the Lord. All these treasure verses tell us that it is because of God's deep love for his children that he disciplines. It is in a sense a confirmation of his love and proof that you belong to him. God disciplines the child he loves (Heb. 12:6). With that said, God's discipline should be welcomed.

One of the most beautiful and heartfelt expressions of this God-given discipline found outside of scripture is that in the poem by John Donne in his Holy Sonnet 14. It reads,

> Batter my heart, three-person'd God, for you
> As yet but knock, breathe, shine, and seek to
>   mend;
> That I may rise and stand, o'erthrow me, and
>   bend
> Your force to break, blow, burn, and make me
>   new.
> I, like an usurp'd town to another due,
> Labor to admit you, but oh, to no end;
> Reason, your viceroy in me, me should defend,
> But is captiv'd, and proves weak or untrue.
> Yet dearly I love you, and would be lov'd fain,

> But am betroth'd unto your enemy;
> Divorce me, untie or break that knot again,
> Take me to you, imprison me, for I,
> Except you enthrall me, never shall be free,
> Nor ever chaste, except you ravish me.

In these fourteen lines, Donne invites God to knock, breathe and shine upon him but also to batter him, overthrow him, bend him, break him, blow him over, and burn him down and even ravish him. He actually welcomes the difficulties that often come with authentic discipline; in that, he knows the outcome will be freedom and chastity. Oh, that we might all feel as did Donne when he wrote this amazing piece of poetic imagery! Have we ever invited God to batter us so that we might break free from our old man nature? Sometimes, that is exactly what it takes. Knock, breathe, and shine on me, oh, God, if it will help me put away my old man!

Of course, it is not the breathing or shining for which we hold such a disdain. It is the knocking we would rather avoid! No one wants the knock! Granted, discipline is never pleasant. Sometimes it hurts. But it can also be just what we need to make progress in our spiritual battle with our old nature. Sometimes it is necessary.

God's methods of discipline aren't exactly quantifiable. They are as varied, infinite, and as creative as are all the other aspects of his nature. I cannot make you a complete list of the ways in which God might choose to discipline you. It is impossible. But I can share with you a few of the more common and very general methods I have seen displayed in others and, most importantly, have experienced in my own life.

Conviction is perhaps the first go to discipline method God might use to get our attention. Holy Spirit conviction. Not to be confused with a guilty conscience, Holy Spirit conviction can be trusted because it doesn't come from our own fallen and sick sense of right and wrong. A simple guilty conscience can be too easily assuaged and convinced of its misappropriated feelings of guilt and shame. Simply put, we can very easily convince ourselves that we are justified in what we have done and that we should not feel guilty. Holy Spirit conviction, on the other hand, originates from God himself and, therefore, will not change its mind on the seriousness of our sin, the cause for this discipline. With God, there is no shadow of turning (James 1:17).

It is one of the roles of the Holy Spirit to convict us of our sin. Jesus told us in John 16:8 that the coming Holy Spirit will "convict the world concerning sin and righteousness and judgement." Likewise, Paul would tell us later in Romans 8:26 that the Spirit "helps us in our weaknesses." So you see, the Holy Spirit both helps us as a preventative to sin, but also as a preventative to repeating that same sin by convicting our hearts and bringing to memory God's truth after the fact. He is first our comforter. Yes, but in order to lead us to comfort he sometimes must bring conviction, which is anything but comfortable.

Spiritual conviction can come in many ways. It can be just a sense in our hearts of guilt and shame over a sin committed. It is a sense we cannot seem to shake. It can also come as a form of remembrance of past lessons learned or experienced, both good and bad. It can also, as has most often been my experience, come as an unending restlessness. This form of conviction results in sleepless nights and lack of productivity and contentment. How many times, my disquiet would have abated sooner if I had only yielded to the conviction of the Holy Spirit! How many times I could have saved myself from much grief and saved precious time if only I had surrendered to this restlessness and repented of said sin sooner rather than later! This restlessness is not a pleasant feeling. It is more than just being tired. It is being unable to find peace.

I have encountered many Christian souls over my years in the ministry seeking counsel for their inability to find peace in their spiritual lives. The sad part of it is just how unnecessary it was for them to go through this period of personal emotional upheaval. All too often, all that was required was for them to simply acknowledge a sin and repent of it in order to end these feelings of foreboding and inner turmoil. For some, it would have meant changing things they weren't ready to change even though they longed for the peace that comes with repentance. This form of spiritual conviction only strengthens the longer we put it off; that is, if we as believers are truly heeding the leading of the Holy Spirit.

Of course, Holy Spirit conviction only comes to those indwelled by the Holy Spirit. For this reason, we shouldn't expect the lost to yield to the Spirit of God. It is for his children that God employs this method of discipline. So the next time you find yourself fighting those feelings of restlessness and finding yourself incapable of truly reaching a rest and contentment; perhaps it is time to ask yourself if there is anything in particular for which you have been ignoring in your heart. Perhaps it is the Holy Spirit keeping you stirred up in order to help you ultimately find true peace!

Other forms of discipline might sometimes accompany this Holy Spirit conviction. Oftentimes, God might simply use consequences to discipline his children. As a parent, I have regularly and simply allowed the natural consequences of certain behaviors be the teacher my children needed. If you do this, then this will happen as a result. Lesson learned. Our heavenly Father also does the same with us.

How many times have we begged and pleaded with God to shield us from the natural consequences of our sinful behavior? Too many, I am afraid. We knew going in what the consequences might be and yet we chose to do it. Then we expect God to just somehow prevent it from playing out as we knew it might. That is our fallen human nature. This response goes all the way back to Eden. Adam and Eve knew exactly what would happen if they chose to disobey and yet they did. We are no different.

Now with that said, we can honestly say that God does sometimes answer our pleas with mercy. He does sometimes shield us from the worst possible consequences of sinful behavior. This usually comes when the guilty person has truly repented and changed the direction of his or her life. Instead of going to prison, a pleading criminal might instead be given a fine or community service. Instead of losing his marriage and family, an adulterer might be shown forgiveness by his wife and kids and his life may not necessarily fall apart. It does happen. But even in those cases where God hears our pleas for mercy and acts accordingly, there are still consequences. For the believer, the consequences might be private spiritual conviction instead of a public denouncement. Nevertheless, there are always consequences, and these consequences are often the tool God uses to discipline us, to change our behaviors moving forward.

But let's be honest. Sometimes spiritual conviction isn't enough. Sometimes we can be so stubborn or committed to our sinful choices that we ignore, or at least try to ignore the leading of the Holy Spirit. We can get so used to the feeling of guilt and shame and restlessness that we simply try to ignore it. The same is true of our consequences. We can be so set in our ways that we just take whatever consequences come our way as being expected and fail to see them as a life-changing, teachable moment. This is dangerous on both accounts. By doing so, we are inviting deeper and more severe forms of conviction and consequences. Sometimes, though, it takes hearing it from someone else. Sometimes discipline comes through others.

God will often use other people to snap us out of our complacency. The right text message at just right time. That phone call or visit that comes just when we need it the most but want it the least. That brother or sister in Christ lovingly and compassionately calling us out on our sin. There is probably nothing more powerful and life-changing than having someone you love and respect coming to you and confronting you about your sin. It reminds me of those old movies from fifty-plus years ago when someone in the story would be in a panic or a rage and would be coming unglued and then someone would grab them by the shoulders and proceed to slap them in the face. That face slap always seemed to bring them back to reality! Well as silly as that seems, every so often that word fitly spoken by someone we love and respect can be like that slap in the face we need to help us see our situation for what it is really. I say this from personal experience.

David has such a friend that God used for his discipline. As we have looked at in previous chapters, David's sin with Bathsheba was one that seemed to snowball and lead him deeper and deeper into sin. He was the king though. Who could discipline the king? Well, God did by sending his prophet to confront David. It wasn't until the prophet Nathan faced him and called him out that David repented and worked to make things right. Nathan was God's disciplinary messenger.

This is one area in which churches have really dropped the ball in the last few decades. There was a time when churches exercised church discipline. They would "bring before the church" those that strayed. Their situation would be discussed and sometimes the truly rebellious would even be "turned out" until such time they repented of their sin. Now there are many problems with this approach, which is probably what led to most churches no longer practicing it. What sin qualifies for church discipline? We all sin, right? Where is the line? I get it. It would make it very easy to slip into legalism and judgmental attitudes. But the original intent was always to lead the sinner to repentance. I feel we have lost something by rejecting the concept of church discipline and authority. Sometimes we need to be called out, not necessarily publicly, but nonetheless with the backing of the authority of scripture and the church. If administered properly as it was in the New Testament church, this form of discipline would be very effective.

Regardless, less formally, God does still send people to us to help us see the error of our ways. For this reason, it is vitally important that believers surround themselves with other likeminded believers who are mature enough in their faith to call us out us when necessary. I speak this from experience. I've had a Christian brother say to me, "What were you thinking?" and then confront me on certain choices I had made. It didn't make me angry. On the contrary, it taught me a lesson and led to my repentance of some pride and arrogance. I feel it was the method God was using to discipline me in that instance. And I thank God for that friend.

Again, there are infinite ways God might choose to discipline you. He is not limited by our understanding of his ways. However it may come, just remember that God's ways of discipline are all administered out of love for you and a desire to see you walk in the freedom that comes with surrendering to his will. He is not out to get you. He is trying to help you.

For the believer, this discipline is inevitable. It is inevitable because we are still sinners. As believers, we are forgiven and justified, but we are still sinners trying to live a life contradictory to our old nature. Therefore, we should expect friction and we should expect God to discipline. It is all part of the adventure of following Christ. And like the poet John Donne quoted earlier in this chapter, we should welcome it. Because through God's discipline we are becoming more and more of the person God sees in us. This knocking, breathing, and shining that God is doing to me is molding me into the person God knows I can be. It may not always be comfortable or pleasant, but through his discipline, I am one step closer to ending the power the old man in the mirror has over me. It is worth it.

So do not be discouraged if you find yourself under the rod and staff of God's disciplining love. What you are going through is not punishment! Discipline is an act of love. It is evidence that you are growing. Most importantly, it is a confirmation that you belong to God.

Looking Even Deeper

Personal/Group Discussion and Application

1. Read Hebrews 12:4–13.

2. What do these verses reveal to us of God's reason for discipline?

3. In your own words, what is the difference between discipline and punishment?

4. Has there ever been a time when you felt as if you were being disciplined by God?

5. What were the methods of discipline in your experiences?

6. What was the result of God's discipline in your experiences and how has it helped in your battle with the old man nature?

7. Pray asking God to help you to avoid his discipline where possible and to accept it where necessary.

10

There Is Nothing Wrong with Vanilla

The perfect church service would be one we were almost
unaware of. Our attention would have been on God.
—C. S. Lewis

Therefore let us be grateful for receiving a kingdom
that cannot be shaken, and thus let us offer to God
acceptable worship, with reverence and awe.
—Hebrews 12:28 (ESV)

I have said it many times, and the older I get, the more I have found
it to be true. It is the simple things in life that give me the greatest
pleasure. Whether it is sitting in the swing with my wife, playing
in the creek with my kids and now my grandkids, wrestling with
my dogs or just going for a walk or eating my favorite dish, there is
nothing more comforting in difficult times than to return to these
simple life affirming activities. It is more than just relaxation. It is
deeper than that. It is just the lack of pretense or complication that
accompany such activities that serve to encourage and strengthen
me. There is no drama. No ulterior motive. Just a plain and simple
returning to what matters most. There is a strength to be found in
simplicity.

Perhaps one of my favorite, if not my all-time favorite deserts,
is a vanilla soft-serve ice cream cone. Yes, there may currently be

thirty-seven or more ever-growing and changing number of available ice cream flavors to be experienced, but sometimes…let's face it… sometimes you just want vanilla. Sometimes you just need vanilla. Vanilla is good. In fact, vanilla is always good. This can't be said of every flavor. None of them can be counted on to faithfully satisfy every time as can vanilla. It is plain. It is simple. But it is delicious! Now, with that image in your mind…if you are still with me and not walking to your freezer…as much as in ice cream, I believe that in all things there is great advantage to be gained and a strength to be found in keeping things simple. This is especially true when we are fighting the good fight and daily battling the old man nature.

In Bible study groups, we often refer to them as "Sunday school answers." They are the answers to discussion questions we often encounter in these study times that seem almost too simple to be true. Or even more, they are so common that they seem to be cliché. Yet they are, nonetheless, true. We should be careful to not dismiss something because it falls under the description of a "Sunday school answer" to a faith-based question. It may very well be that it has achieved this "Sunday school answer" status because it has been proven to be a trustworthy answer to a difficult question time and time again over the course of many years. Such answers might include simple truths such as pray, read your Bible, and go to church.

You see, we could answer almost any Christian living type question with one of these three answers. They are the vanilla answers to our deeper theological questions. Simple enough, yet still true. However, the average teacher often wishes for more depth than these answers from their students. I know I do. But simple or not, arising from deep thought and reflection or just the opposite, it doesn't make them any less true or any less important. If we are honest, we must admit that these concepts are indeed the best answers to many of life's challenges.

Along with everything we have been discussing thus far in this book, there are still a few more tools we can use to equip us for the battle against our flesh and old self. Sunday school answers or not, to truly set our mind on things above and less on things of this world, the most effective methods are still the simplest. Among these simple strengthening methods are the disciplines of worship and Bible study, acts of service and, of course, prayer.

This reality is why we have the local church. While church attendance is not necessary to carry out these simple disciplines, we do find them all occurring there and as such it does exist to equip us and encourage us and to provide the means for us to make them part of our everyday life. We can pray at home and should. We can study our Bible at home, and we should. We can worship anywhere and at any time, and we should. Our acts of Christian service are not limited to church work in the traditional sense. Nevertheless, the institution of church exists to motivate us, prepare us, and empower us to truly live these Sunday school answers, not just know about them.

The biblical church helps us to make these truths part of who we are, not just part of what we know. It is for this reason we are told to "forsake not meeting together as some are in habit of doing" (Heb. 10:25). We need the church. It is one of the many weapons God has given us to wield in our fight against the old man nature. Yes, as Christians, we are the church. It is not the building or the meeting schedule. Nevertheless, the local church is the means by which our beliefs are strengthened and expressed.

I will not go so far as to say that spiritual growth cannot exist in one that doesn't attend church. But let's be honest? Does it? Even if it does, how much slower is it and how do we even know if we are going in the right direction without having other believers off of which to bounce our thoughts and questions? Plus, and most importantly, we are instructed in scripture to attend the local church. Again, see Hebrews 10:25 and follow the references in your Bible. We are told to be actively a part of a local body of believers. By doing so, we help meet the needs of others by using our gifts and talents and by fulfilling our part in the fellowship. We are one body made up of many necessary parts (1 Cor. 12). When we are out, a part is missing, and church is less effective. But it is not just for the wellbeing of others that we attend, it is for our own good as well. The church helps us to grow stronger. Simple but true.

I have had many a church member over the years attest to me of how they can worship anywhere and at any time, usually saying as such after having missed a Sunday or two. It seems that here in the deep south, I hear this most often during the fishing and hunting seasons and during the summer vacations. Can you worship on the back of a bass boat? Yes. Can you worship while trout fishing on the banks of the Chattahoochee River coming down from the Blue Ridge Mountains? Yes. Can you worship on the white beaches of the Gulf of Mexico? Yes. And I have experienced many personal worship experiences in those settings. But for that to happen, it must be intentional. If we are sincere, we should admit that most of these times we are more concerned with hooking that next big fish or seeing that next big deer or avoiding that sunburn more so than worship, Bible study, or reflecting on God's goodness. At best, our minds and hearts are divided in those moments. Genuine worship requires an undivided and attentive heart. As the C. S. Lewis quote at the beginning of this chapter implies, the truest worship occurs when God has our full and entire attention. He deserves no less.

True worship happens when we close our minds and heart to the worries of the world and focus our all in all on the giver of all good things. It is when we look fully to our God. To do that means our minds are not on that temptation we are fighting or on those feelings of shame and guilt that our old man would have us to focus upon. It is for this reason that worship is a powerful instrument to use in our battle. It is all part of that reckoning ourselves dead to sin and alive to Christ that we looked at in chapter 6. It is changing our focus from self to God. The more we do it, the more ground we gain in our struggle.

This is true whether the worship is corporate as in our Sunday morning services or perhaps personally as one might experience on your back porch or on the back of a lawn mower. Yes, some of my greatest prayer times and even some of my best sermons came to me while cutting my grass. Beneath the roar of that mower engine, I am able to push out all other distractions and focus. Worship is about focus. If our focus is on God, it is off ourselves.

Our old man grows weaker each time we worship. When engaged in the struggle with the old-man nature, honest worship is like ignoring the bully in the room in favor of your best friend.

Ignoring him drains him of his power over you and builds up your friend's influence instead.

This old-self nature, along with our enemy, will always try to distract you from worship, both corporate and personal. How many times have you found yourself thinking about Sunday dinner or something else when you should be lifting your voices and hearts to the Lord in worship or meditating on scripture? How many times have you been distracted by everyday life when you have intentionally set time aside for personal worship? It is because worship is a threat to the old man and to the old enemy. They can't stand to be ignored because when we ignore them and turn our hearts to God, we take away their power. The bully's teeth are pulled. Worship makes us stronger and our enemies weaker. Most importantly, though, genuine worship glorifies God. When God is glorified, everything else is put in its place.

Along with worship and Bible study, another simple tool we can use in the putting away of our old self is the discipline of service. This can certainly be done through the local church but is not limited to church work as we think of it. It occurs any time we follow the teachings of Christ and put the needs of others ahead of ourselves. It happens when we give of our time, talents, and treasure to help others. Again, by doing so, we are taking the focus off of ourselves.

Over the years, I have served as a pastor. I have counseled many a discouraged believer. One of the best defenses against discouragement and depression I have seen is for them get their minds off themselves and to look to help others. An easy way to do this is to engage in some form of Christian service. When our concerns move from self to others, our own issues seem smaller. They are not necessarily smaller, but they seem so because we no longer are fixated on them. Combine this with worship and prayer and we are that much stronger. And the old man is that much weaker.

In Matthew 20:28, we are told that "Even as the Son of Man came not to be served but to serve." Even Jesus, King of kings and Lord of lords, made it his priority to serve others. His very existence was one of service and sacrifice. He was born to live and die for others. This example is for all of us to follow.

This service-driven mindset is one thing that made Jesus so different from all the religious leaders of his day as well as setting him apart from the many other men who had falsely claimed to be messiah. They were in it for themselves. They wanted fame and power. Jesus did not seek this kind of notoriety. In fact, many times in his early ministry years, Jesus asked the people he had helped or healed to not be saying publicly who they thought he was. He wasn't seeking that kind of power-driven praise even though he was the one person in all existence that deserved it. When the world was expecting a conquering and powerful military-type messiah, Jesus gave them a suffering servant. Over two thousand years later, we don't know hardly any of the names of the others, but we still worship Jesus of Nazareth and his name is world-renowned. His message of serving others changed the world.

Today, that same message still changes lives. To serve others means you are not serving yourself. The spiritual irony occurs in that by serving others we are still helping ourselves. Anyone involved in any form of mission work or service can attest to this truth. It is life-changing. We become stronger, and our old man becomes weaker every time we do something selflessly for others. It is incredibly effective in helping us gain the advantage over our old man nature. It helps us stay humble and consequently allows God more room to work in our hearts.

Both worship and service, whether through the local church or through my own personal efforts, are all dependent on the last of the three simple Sunday school answers. Prayer is the most powerful part of our arsenal in our fight against the old man. Prayer, of course, encompasses all parts of our Christian life. It involves everything.

First Thessalonians 5:17 instructs us to "Pray without ceasing." The implication of this verse is that we are to always be ready to pray. We are to be in constant communication with God. In other words, we are to be talking to God all throughout our day. It is to be as natural to speak with him as it is to speak with one another, a spouse or a close friend, maybe even more so, in that, there is nothing about us that he does not know. There is no time we can't pray and nothing we can't say. God wants this kind of open and heartfelt communing with his children.

Praying for the strength to withstand the temptation to follow the old man should be our first go to act of resistance, not our last-ditch effort. Praying for the strength to resist is not only communicating with God; it is also acknowledging that you need a strength beyond your own in order to gain ground. It too is in a sense an act of worship.

Unfortunately, prayer has become the topic of so many social media memes and the like that many fail to see the power of it. How many times do we casually say, "I'll pray for you" or "My prayers are with you" when someone is struggling for any number of reasons? How many times do we answer a text message with a praying hands emoji and then never follow through with an actual prayer? In fact, it has become such a colloquialism for so many in our modern culture that even nonbelievers utter the words without even thinking about what they really mean. For them, prayer is nothing more than well-wishing or sending positive thoughts your way. But for the believer, it is much more than that! Prayer is bending the very ear of God almighty to my lips. It is asking him to fight on my behalf. It is tapping into the strength and wisdom of the creator of the universe. It is not to be confused with somehow manipulating or using God's power for our own benefit. It is communicating with our God. It is a child seeking the attention of their father. It is a natural part of our relationship with him.

Prayer is to the believer as breathing is to any living creature. It is necessary to life. Prayer opens doors and shuts doors. Prayer frees the prisoner both literal and figuratively. Prayer strengthens us and weakens our enemies. Prayer pushes our old man to the background and brings God to the foreground. Prayer makes us stronger. For this reason, prayer is to be part of our worship, service, and our everyday living. Prayer helps us keep all things in perspective. Prayer is simple enough to do, yet more than able to tear down great strongholds. It is simple, strong, and all-encompassing.

These Sunday school solutions to life's greatest struggles have become so well accepted because they are so valuable and because they work. Don't let the trite way we handle them blind you to their efficacy. As the old saying goes, "If it ain't broke, don't fix it." These things aren't broken. They work because they take our minds and hearts away from self and point them in the right direction.

In John 3:30, the cousin and predecessor to Christ, John the Baptist, made a profound statement. When speaking of Jesus beginning his earthly ministry, John addressed some of the concerns of his own jealous followers with the statement "He must increase, but I must decrease." The NIV reads, "He must become greater, I must become less." While we must consider this passage in its historical context, the principle behind the Baptist's statement remains a sound one for all of us to follow. God must increase in our lives and the self must decrease.

This is desperately true if we are to have victory over our old man nature. *The self cannot be defeated by the self!* To overcome self, we need something bigger, stronger, and originating from without our own being. We need God. All the methods mentioned in this book recognize that need and lead us to the remedy of that need. They bring us closer to God and further from self. They help God to increase and the self to decrease.

To gain the victory over the old man, there are many things to consider and many things we can do. That is what every chapter in this book details. Nevertheless, sometimes the most potent way to do something is to return to the things we learned at first, the simple and true things. Simple prayer, worship, service, and church have always been and will always be among the most powerful weapons we can harness in our fight. Do not neglect them. Do not underestimate them. Use them as the weapons for which they are intended. Find in them the strength of simplicity.

Remember, there is nothing wrong with vanilla. Vanilla is good.

Looking Even Deeper

Personal/Group Discussion and Application

1. Read Revelation 2:5.

2. In this passage written about and to the church at Ephesus, God instructs the church to repent and return to the things they did at first. How can neglecting these simple "firsts" effect our spiritual growth? How did they affect the church at Ephesus?

3. What are some more "Sunday school answers" to the struggle of overcoming our old man nature that perhaps the author didn't cover in this chapter?

4. How does true worship give us strength for the fight?

5. How does serving others give us strength for the fight?

6. Do you agree with the author that you cannot defeat self with self? How so?

7. Pray that God will give you ever increasing opportunities and desire to pray, serve and worship.

11

FAR FROM NORMAL

Jesus promised his disciples three things—that they would be completely fearless, absurdly happy, and in constant trouble.
—*William Barclay*

Indeed, all who desire to live a godly life in
Christ Jesus will be persecuted.
—2 Timothy 3:12

On the day that you decide to follow your new nature, you should expect someone, perhaps someone close to you to question your sincerity and even think that you are acting strangely. One would think that pursuing a life of holiness would please those that are closest to us. In most cases, it does. However, it has been my experience as a pastor and as a fellow struggling Christian that there will be those that for whatever reason cannot or will not believe it. Perhaps, it is because they know our past so well or perhaps it is because they know their own. Regardless as to why, to truly commit to following Christ in our life is to invite personal scrutiny. We shouldn't be surprised by it. We should expect it. You may be praised for it and you may also be seen as a unique and odd anomaly.

Jesus warned us that this would be the case all throughout the gospels. He did not shy away from warning us of persecution. Luke 6:22, Matthew 5:10–12, John 15:18 are a few examples. There are also many warnings in the epistles as well such as 2 Timothy 3:12, 2 Corinthians 12:10, and many others. Peter also told us that we shouldn't be surprised when trials come upon us. It is a regular part of the Christian experience.

Of course, the purpose of this chapter is not so much about persecution. Persecution occurs. It is real. But I am not sure that what I am getting at here could be considered persecution so much as it is more of a kind of disrespect or personal skepticism. Some people have a hard time when someone close to them chooses to get serious about their faith. They simply cannot accept it. And there will probably be that person in your life as you make wanted changes that will have no problem sharing their opinion on the subject with you. Whenever you commit to spiritual growth, there will always be naysayers saying it can't be done or that you aren't really serious about what God is calling you to do. It hurts, and it probably falls short of the definition of persecution. But it still hurts.

I learned this lesson myself early on in my spiritual walk. When I first surrendered to God's calling on my life to full-time Christian ministry, I had several people try to talk me out of it. These were Christian people that I loved and respected and they tried to convince me that I had misunderstood God's calling on my life. Then when I followed through a couple of years later and enrolled in college to pursue my calling, there were then others that piled on and encouraged me to seek another degree so that I might have a "backup" plan should "this ministry thing" not work out. I always felt as if for them it was more a question of when than if it didn't work out. I also had lifelong Christian friends that began to act strange around me as if my desire to follow God's will for my life somehow changed me. If anything, I felt as if it had changed them.

But it didn't end there. A year or so ago at a family reunion, I had someone whom I have known my whole life ask me what I was doing with myself these days. I began to speak to them of my church and ministries and their response was "Oh yeah, that's right. You are a preacher, right?"

Yeah. I am a preacher. And I have been one for nearly thirty years now! It's all that I've ever been! I've never wanted to do or be anything else. I've been around this person many times during those years. During this time, I've preached all over the part of the state in which they live in both churches and other events, I have written books, I've been in the local news, in denominational news, I have earned four corresponding college degrees, received an honorary doctorate, and performed more funerals, weddings, and baptisms in the area than I can count. (Again, imagine me patting myself on the back somewhat self-righteously right now. Thank you.) Yet after more than three decades of full-time ministry, some of my family still can't see me as anything other than that young shy boy that I was all those years ago. A pastor? Yeah, right. Not likely.

Why is that? Why can't they just see that God had a plan for me and I followed it? People do that you know. Don't get me wrong. I am not bitter over this. It's almost become like a joke to me now. But it hasn't always been that way. When I was struggling most with my commitment in those early years, I didn't need close friends and family doubting my seriousness. I needed their support. Don't get me wrong; most did support me, but those few that didn't really stand out in my mind. It hurt. I've forgiven them, but it did hurt, nonetheless.

Well, it doesn't only happen to preachers and those called to full-time Christian vocation. It can happen to any believer who is seriously striving to make a change in their life. It most definitely happens when we are determined to stand up against our old nature and pursue a life of holiness that's pleasing to God. It seems the world around us likes to join with the old man and remind us of its remaining presence in our lives and our past mistakes. The idea of growth or change is almost always met with resistance from our old self, our relations, and definitely our enemy.

Again, Jesus warned us that it might happen this way. He even went so far as to tell us that he didn't come to bring us peace, but division (Luke 12:51). Wait a minute! What about peace on Earth, good will toward men that we sing about at his birth? Well, he did bring us peace with God and peace of heart and mind through the forgiveness of our sins and our justification. But when it comes to our relationships, our faith sometimes causes division. It might even bring division in the home.

Even Jesus's family couldn't bring themselves to accept what he was doing or believe in him (John 7:5). Should we expect any different? When we get serious about our faith, we should get ready for someone to openly doubt our sincerity or at best to lovingly disagree, perhaps someone close. However, we cannot let this reality rob us of our determination to put the old man behind us.

The best thing we can do during these times of personal scrutiny is to press on. It comes down to this simple question. Are we going to listen to the naysayers or are we going to follow God? Who knows best, the world or the creator of the world, the world I live in or the one who created me to live in the world? To put the old man behind us, we must keep the Son of Man in front of us.

There is a story in the Old Testament that I simply love. It is one of those hidden treasures that can easily be overlooked when reading the Old Testament historical accounts. We read through the action of the story so fast that we miss the significance of the words. It involves one my favorite Old Testament heroes, David, and it contains a life-changing precept. It is found in 2 Samuel 5:4–7.

> David was thirty years old when he became king, and he reigned forty years. In Hebron he reigned over Judah seven years and six months, and in Jerusalem he reigned over all Israel and Judah thirty-three years. The king and his men marched to Jerusalem to attack the Jebusites, who lived there. The Jebusites said to David, "You will not get in here; even the blind and the lame can ward you off." They thought, "David cannot get in here." Nevertheless, David captured the fortress of Zion—which is the City of David.

This event occurs in the very first days of David's reign as king over Israel. He was thirty years old and had just been crowned king. It had been many years since Samuel had first anointed David and prophesied that he would be the next king of Israel. Ironically on that day, not even David's father Jesse had enough confidence in David to bring him out of the field to stand with his brothers for Samuel to see when he had come to name one of his sons as the next king (1 Sam. 16). It appears that David experienced the same thing we are talking about here in this chapter. Of all his brothers, no one even considered that he might be the one Samuel was looking for nor thought enough of him to even call him out of the field where he was tending the sheep. Yet surprise, this shepherd boy was the one God was looking for. It would be years before David would see that anointing fulfilled, but it would come to pass.

David would have to go through many trials before he would rise to the position of king. He would have to slay a giant named Goliath, fight many battles, and flee from a jealous King Saul for years. During these events, he would pen some of the most beautiful psalms contained in our canon of scripture. With all his faults, King David would forever be known as a man after God's own heart. But his standing with God wasn't always recognized by those around him, as we see in the abovementioned account from 2 Samuel 5.

In the story, David's first act as new king was to go to Jerusalem, which at the time was occupied by the Jebusites. Upon David's arrival, he found the city occupied and the walls and gates secure. As he and his men stood outside the walls looking at this seemingly insurmountable and impenetrable task ahead of them, the enemy was hurling insults down from atop the wall. Sound familiar? They said basically, "You can't do this. Even our lame and blind could defend us against you." Wow! They simply didn't know who they were really up against.

I love verse 7. In a matter-of-fact, nonchalant manner, God includes a word in verse 7 that has come to mean a lot to me. Nevertheless. All the enemy's men are doubting King David and insulting him and his efforts and then… "Nevertheless, David captured the stronghold of Zion, that is the City of David." They said he couldn't. Nevertheless, he did. You see, they miscalculated. They didn't know what David knew. They didn't know that it was God doing the fighting for him. What man can't do, God always can.

They said he couldn't. Nevertheless.

When you get serious about living for the Lord and living as a person freed from their old nature, expect the opposing voices to say it can't be done. When it happens, say to yourself…nevertheless!

The old man nature will tell you there is no point in trying. Nevertheless!

Others will tell you that you aren't serious. Nevertheless!

Your spiritual enemy will tell you it is of no use to even try. Nevertheless!

Like David, you can have your own nevertheless moment. With God's help, the expectations of others can be silenced, and victory can be won. Even if the opposing voices are not silenced, God will give you the confidence to simply ignore them and let him do through you what he does best. He will give you your own nevertheless moment.

For the believer, it is more a question of accepting our new reality. We are no longer slaves to our old self. (See chapter 6.) As believers indwelled by the Holy Spirit, we aren't limited by our human weaknesses. He that indwells us greater than all (1 John 4:4). Also, as believers we are constantly in a state of change and growth. To desire this change isn't the exception. It isn't strange or weird. It is to be the norm. To not be in a state of change is the exception in the kingdom of God. We are to always be changing and growing more and more into the image of Christ.

The world would have us to believe that we are products of our genetics or upbringing, and that change is unlikely and futile at best. How many times have we heard statements like these? I was born this way. I was raised this way. Or my favorite… It is just the way I am. The implications of these statements are that change is not likely and perhaps even unusual. So when we try to change…here come the pessimists ready to throw a wet blanket on all our efforts. Our desire to change is seen by them as abnormal. Well, as Christians living in this fallen and troubled world, we are called to be anything but normal. We are to be different and have distinct values.

The body of Christ is made up of people from all walks of life. It includes goofy people, overly serious people, emotional people, smart people, and yes, even weird people, all held together with one loving, compassionate, and merciful glue, Jesus Christ. The body of Christ is far from what the world considers normal. Again, these differences will invite people to look at your spiritual growth and give you the inevitable "yeah, right." They will question your sincerity because they do not understand it themselves. And that is okay. As with David, they will be telling you to stay in your field or standing on the wall and saying you can't do it. Nevertheless! God knows different.

By the world's standards, your desire to be more like Christ is not normal and, therefore, hard to accept. But the world noticing your change should not be seen as insult or persecution. Sure, we all like to be respected and to have our growth recognized, especially by those closest to us. But it simply doesn't always happen. Accept this reality and you will be much happier and, therefore, enjoy more successes in your battle with the old man nature.

In a sense, these outward doubts pointed at you can be seen as a compliment. It means you are far from the normal of the world. It means you are different. It is hard, but try to not take the doubts of others personal. Instead take them as a confirmation that you are shining a light in a dark world. Take them as confirmation that you are moving in the right direction.

To be far from normal is to be close to God. To be doubted by the world is to be like Jesus. To be far from normal is to set yourself up for your very own "nevertheless" moment of victory. So ignore the naysayers and let God work in you and he will also work through you.

Remember… Nevertheless!

Looking Even Deeper

Personal/Group Discussion and Application

1. Read Luke 12:51–53.

2. These are strong words of Christ. What are the implications for all believers in these words?

3. Has there ever been an instance in your life when others doubted your sincerity or faith? How did it make you feel? How did you respond?

4. What are some ways Christians are to be different than the world?

5. Would you say that others see you as normal or different? Why is that?

6. Give an example of a time when God has shown himself faithful to you even when others doubted? Share a nevertheless moment.

7. Pray for God to give you the courage to follow him even when others doubt or try to stop you.

12

Eating the Elephant

Do you mortify; do you make it your daily work; be always at it whilst you live; cease not a day from this work; be killing sin or it will be killing you.

—John Owen

As it is said, "Today, if you hear his voice, do not harden your hearts as in the rebellion."

—Hebrews 3:15

As you are reading this book, you are probably feeling somewhat overwhelmed. You are considering all we have looked at and are probably thinking, *How can I ever achieve victory? How will I ever kill my old man?* It is a herculean task, and I am but a weak and broken person. Well, that is good. If that is truly how you feel, then you are heading in the right direction and better off than most. It is in humility that God will lead you to victory.

If you read this and come away thinking, *Well, I've got this. Look out old man…here I come.* Then you are setting yourself up for disappointment with your pride, and you will soon be back in front of that mirror facing the old man once again. It is only with God's help that your old nature will be put in its place. To try to overcome by your own strength is a works-based pseudo faith promoted by the old self, and it is only by God's free and unmerited grace that we can have the daily strength we need to slowly chip away at the old man's influence. We are saved by grace, and we stand each day by grace.

With that said, it is still a big undertaking ahead of you and the overpowering feelings you might be having right now are to be expected. But you do not have to drown in this deluge of emotions. My purpose in writing this book was to help free you from the stress and burden of fighting the old man, not lay further weight upon you. For this reason, you must not allow it to become a load, but instead see it as an opportunity for God to work. The tools we have looked at in this book will hopefully help you in the fight. Nevertheless, you must also know that it will not happen overnight. The end of the old man fight is always in our future. It is too much to accomplish in one day or in a few days. It takes time. It takes a lifetime.

So how do we proceed?

Well, there is a joke that I have often used that is fitting. I guess you would call it a joke. I am not sure if I would; in that, the truth it illustrates is one of such spiritual importance. It asks this riddle. How do you eat an elephant? The answer…one bite at a time.

That is how we must defeat our old man. He is the elephant. We eat him one bite at a time. We defeat him one small victory at a time. We beat him now, and tomorrow, we may face him again. We live the Christian life and fight the Christian fight one day at a time. It is a process, and it doesn't happen all at once. It takes a lifetime to kill our old man.

As you read the scriptures, you will find many verses that imply an urgency when it comes to the gospel message and to the value of living our faith out daily. Today is the day of your salvation (2 Cor. 6:2). This is the day the Lord has made (Ps. 118:24). Today if you hear his voice (Heb. 3:7). Exhort one another while it is still called today (Heb. 3:13). Even Jesus himself when teaching us to pray told us to pray for our daily bread (Matt. 6:9–13). Today seems to be a moment of singular significance to our Lord. Not tomorrow. Not yesterday. Today is what seems to matter most. Perhaps it is because this moment is really all we have.

In his book *The Holiest of All*, the great Christian author of years gone by, Andrew Murray refers to this urgency as the "ever-present now." We never reach tomorrow, and we cannot return to yesterday. We are always in the here and now. In this ever-present now we can live for Christ. In the ever-present now, we can choose to be the new creation and not follow the leanings of the old man nature. In the ever-present now, we can kill our old man. The ever-present now is my opportunity to take a small bite out of the gargantuan elephant.

This is important because later today, I may choose otherwise. I may fail and instead choose to follow the old man. Tomorrow I may take another bite out of the elephant, or it may take a bite out of me. Each day holds its own challenges. Again, this is why Jesus told us to let tomorrow worry about itself and instead focus on today (Matt. 6:34). He was challenging us to live in the ever-present now. This moment is the only moment we can change. This moment is the only moment we can actually live.

You see, the fight against the old man nature is not one of complete earthly victory or defeat. We have to stop looking at it as a pass-or-fail kind of test. We will look at the complete victory more in the next chapter. It is instead more of a question of victory or defeat in this moment. It is the only moment we can control. It is not about score keeping as much as it is about direction. The small victories in the ever-present now is what we should be striving for. The more often it happens, the further and further apart the setbacks will be and the more assurance we will have that we are moving in the right direction. This war is ultimately won by a series of small victories. The elephant is eaten one bite at a time.

What does this mean for us practically? We are dead to sin. We are dead to self. We have crucified the old man. Why can't we have a once and for all victory? Well, we are dead to it, but it is not yet dead. Again, I refer you to the earlier chapters. We have been given a new nature. Our old nature still exists. We are no longer a slave to it, but it is still there. So all we can do is what we can do right now. All we can do is choose this moment to live for Christ. So practically speaking, we should only concern ourselves with the ever-present now.

Our past has been forgiven. If we have repented and sought God's forgiveness, there is really nothing else we can do about our past. That is okay. God is through with it. We should be too. He has told us that our sins have been cast behind his back, out of sight and out of mind (Isa. 38:17). He remembers them no more (Heb. 10:17). The Bible is filled with verses that promise us that God not only forgives us of our sins but forgets about them all together. I challenge you to do an internet search of Bible verses that speak of God's forgiveness. You will be amazed at the hundreds of verses that speak of his forgiveness and his corresponding *forgetfulness*. Our past only becomes a hindrance in our relationship with God if we fail to repent of it or if we simply fail to let it go. Put simply, it can only distract us if we hold on to it. God has let it go. We need too as well. We cannot change it. But thanks to God and his forgiving and merciful nature, we don't have to. The past of the born-again blood bought believer doesn't matter in the ever-present now.

Likewise, our "never-present" future is also impossible to manage. It is for God alone to know. We do not know what our future holds. We do not know what temptations we will be facing in what for us is an undetermined future. Only God knows. All we can do is trust in him and prepare ourselves so that we will be best equipped to face it when it comes. When it comes, however, it is no longer our future. It is then our ever-present now. The future is still ahead. It is never present. Even though our future dreams are filled with hope and promise; we cannot live in the future.

The always here and ever-present now is all we have!

Even if we have failed a million times and allowed the old self to guide our choices in the past, and even if we want a future free of its influence, the only moment in which we can make a difference is this one. And this one moment may very well change the entire direction of my life. That is, of course, assuming we have repented of past sins. If you have repented and you have successfully put away the old man in this current moment, then you are moving in the same direction you would have been had you not failed to do so the last time. Read that sentence again if you need too. How far along you are on the journey is not nearly important as is the direction you are traveling. God will honor our efforts if we are seeking to follow him, no matter how far along we may have progressed.

The problem with eating the elephant whole is that you can get easily discouraged and stop trying to clean your plate. It is a lot to swallow all at once. Trying to kill our old man once and for all is no different. To attempt to kill him once and for all will only leave you discouraged and possibly so discouraged that you stop trying. It is an unrealistic expectation. God does not expect us too. That is why he places such an emphasis on today in his word. Again, today is what should matter the most.

God knows you will fail from time to time. None of this catches him by surprise or changes the status of your relationship with him. Thankfully, his love for you is not based on performance. It is based on his grace. As believers, we do not have a performance-based identity. We have a grace-based identity.

So if you are feeling overwhelmed with the thought of fighting the old man nature that has been such a nuisance to you for such a long time, then just slow down and take a breath. Instead of trying to swallow it whole, just slow down and take a small bite. Don't worry about cleaning your plate. Eat what is right in front of you and leave the rest for tomorrow.

Choose this moment to put the old man aside and follow the leading of the Holy Spirit in the ever-present now. Fight him in this moment. Don't worry about last time and don't stress over what you will do next time. Seize this moment. Pray. Worship. Repent. Pray some more. Do what you must in order to win this particular present battle. The war is not won or lost in a day. Focus instead on this battle. This is the moment that counts. Don't let it get away. Win this moment. Put him aside in the here and now. It is all that matters.

Looking Even Deeper

Personal/Group Discussion and Application

1. Read Ephesians 5:14–21.

2. What are some examples in this Ephesians passage of ways to make the most of ever-present now?

3. Do you ever struggle with letting go of the past? Why is that?

4. In your own experience, what happens when you focus too much on what you cannot change?

5. What are some practical ways you can put aside your old man today?

6. Pray asking God to give you strength for the ever-present now and to leave the never present future in his hands.

13

A Better Country

If I find in myself a desire which no experience in
this world can satisfy, the most probable explanation
is that I was made for another world.

—C. S. Lewis

But as it is, they desire a better *country*, that is, a
heavenly one. Therefore God is not ashamed to be called
their God; for He has prepared a city for them.

—Hebrews 11:16 (NASB)

The fact that the battle never ends between the spirit and the flesh,
between the old nature and the new nature, leaves us with this question. Where is the hope? What possible advantage is there for me to
keep fighting a fight that I most likely will not win? What possible
benefit is there to being a Christian if in this life all it means is that I
will be in constant conflict with my old man?

Well, first I have not said that you will not win the war. In fact,
it is already won. The war has already been won for us by Jesus. One
day, our old man will die. It is a guaranteed win. His days are num-
bered. But until the day our war is over, there are battles to be fought.
As far as the battles go, you will win some and you will lose some.
The conflict, however, will not be constant.

As we saw in the last chapter, the more battles you win, the greater the down time will be between the battles. And with each new victory will come a great joy and satisfaction. The fact that we will always be fighting our old man nature this side of heaven does not imply that we will always feel the sting of defeat. On the contrary, hopefully you have now gained a better understanding of the fight and likewise gained some weapons to use in your fight. It is my prayer that this book will help your fight get easier and easier as the years go by and that you will have extended periods of spiritual success and respite.

One thing that will still assist you in your fight, though, is for you to remember that the complete, total, and final victory you have yet to experience is already yours. Jesus won it for you on the cross and more importantly by leaving behind that empty borrowed tomb. The resurrection was not just Jesus's victory, but ours as well.

In his first epistle, John tells us in 1 John 5:4, "For everyone who has been born of God overcomes the world. And this is the victory that has overcome the world—our faith." Through Jesus, the world has been overcome, and subsequently, we already have the victory we so desperately seek. The war is won. The battles leading up to that point are all that's left. It is just something we must go through before we enjoy the eternal victory celebration.

A day will come when we will no longer have to fight. Our existence will be one of no more pain, no more tears and no more struggles (Rev. 21:4). Most importantly, it will be an existence with no more sin! Our old man will be left behind and all that will remain will be the resurrected new creation. It will truly and literally be heaven. It is more than just our final destination. It is our home. It is our longing. It is our hope.

In J. R. R. Tolkien's classic *The Lord of the Rings*, there is a conversation between two of the main characters Gandalf and Pippin that touch on this longing. The conversation took place on the eve of a great battle. They were facing impossible odds defending Middle Earth and did not expect to survive. Knowing what awaited him in just a few short hours, the little hobbit named Pippin was pondering his existence and it's inevitable and unpleasant expected end and struck up this conversation with the white wizard Gandalf. It goes as follows:

> PIPPIN: I didn't think it would end this way.
> GANDALF: End? No, the journey doesn't end here. Death is just another path, one that we all must take. The grey rain-curtain of this world rolls back, and all turns to silver glass, and then you see it.
> PIPPIN: What? Gandalf? See what?
> GANDALF: White shores, and beyond, a far green country under a swift sunrise.
> PIPPIN: Well, that isn't so bad.
> GANDALF: No. No, it isn't."

What beautiful imagery is painted in this description of our heavenly home! It is what we as believers long for! A place where sin no longer has a hold on us. A silvery sea with a white shore and green country beyond. A place of sheer peace and beauty. Is it worth the wait? Is it worth the struggle? Gandalf seemed to think so. So do I!

The apostle Peter refers to believers as "aliens and strangers" in his letter to the church (1 Pet. 2:11). The implications of that passage and others like it is that children of God are not at home here in this mortal existence. As followers of Christ, we will always struggle to live in this temporary dwelling place. It is to be expected. It is to be expected because we no longer belong here. Our home is behind that grey rain-curtain of this world and on those white shores and the green country beyond.

While still living here, there will be always outward friction with the locals and inward friction with the old man nature. This is true for as long as we dwell in a land that is not ours. It is for this reason that the author of Hebrews, most often considered to be Paul, spoke of the longing felt by the Old Testament patriarchs. As seen at the beginning of this chapter, in Hebrews 11:6, he mentions the great heroes of Hebrews 11 as looking forward to "a better country." This longing helped them to navigate the temporary discomforts of their sojourning. They could tolerate the hardships of life in a strange land because they knew their home was yet to come and that it would be one free of fighting and trouble. These momentary troubles will only last for a short while when viewed through the eyes and timeline of eternity (2 Cor. 4:17). This is the hope of the Christian faith and one of the most distinct differences between the believer and the rest of the world.

The reality of our heavenly home is a great source of strength in our fight against the old man nature. It takes the pressure off. For us the fight is not a make-or-break fight because we are saved by grace through faith (Eph. 2:8–9). The victory has already been achieved by Jesus and his resurrection. Through him, we have won and we will know what it means to win. Our rate of success in our daily fights against the self does not qualify us or disqualify us for admittance to the better country of Hebrews 11. The fight is important, vitally important to a life of peace and contentment here until such an appointed time that we must leave this home for our next, but it does not open or close the door on our heavenly home. In fact, we can face the trials of this world and this life knowing that even as we speak our heavenly home is being prepared for us by Jesus himself (John 14:3). And it is going to be a beauty.

I'll never forget the day my wife and I bought our current home. We had been looking at a few other houses and dreaming about what our new home might look like. We had seen this house online and wanted to see it in person, but before we could arrange it with our realtor, the house went under contract. We thought it had been lost forever. However, it soon came back on the market. The other contract had fallen through. So we made a call and the next day we toured the home in person.

We knew almost immediately that it was the home we wanted. We liked the house, and it was the right price. It was an older construction but had been remodeled and had everything we wanted. The deal clincher for me was the property on which it was situated. To make it even more appealing, the very private property had almost six acres of hardwood trees on a small mountain like setting. It even had a stream. I fell in love with it immediately and so did my wife. So we made an offer and a few weeks later we moved in.

The house had been vacant for a while and the unattended yard had slowly given way to the encroaching adjacent woods. The surrounding brush had grown so thick that you couldn't even see the house from the road. It would be a great deal of work to get the yard to the condition I would like to see it. (I'll let you know when it happens.) It took me and my family weeks to clear off the bank in front of the home just so you could see the house from the road. Four years later and I am still working on the yard and making improvements to the house to make it our dream home. I imagine I will be doing the same four years from now. In fact, I hope to be doing so forty years from now. I think it will be a never-ending endeavor.

The reality of this futile though enjoyable work is this: no matter how hard I work on transforming this house into our dream home, one day it will belong to someone else. Most likely, I will leave it to my kids, and they will do what they will with it. Eventually, it might very well belong to someone completely different and not even connected with my family.

I am reminded of this truth every time I walk down my long driveway. At the end of my driveway, there are two names written into the cement. One is *Charlotte* and the other is *Andy*. Apparently, they owned the home when the cement driveway was poured, and they wrote their names into the wet cement as a permanent memorial. From what records I can find, they also built the house. They have since died, and having no heirs, what must have once been their dream home became the property of the state and later auctioned off and sold to an investment company. They then remodeled it and then sold it to me. All that now remains of Charlotte and Andy in this place is their names scribbled in the cement at the end of my driveway. One day, all that will remain of me and my wife in this place will be the temporary changes we have made. Someone may come behind me and erase those as well. This is the nature of our earthly existence.

But for the believer, this is not all there is to our existence. There are many intangible legacies we can leave behind. The things that matter most are the things not inscribed in cement but inscribed on the hearts of the people we love. These are inscriptions of eternal significance. This is why the fight with our old man is not futile. It has a purpose. It not only makes us stronger, more like Christ and more at peace, but it testifies to the life-changing power of Jesus to others. The harder I fight the good fight, the deeper the inscription will be on the hearts of my kids, grandkids, and friends. My failures won't be recorded, but my successes will be engraved on the hearts of my family and friends.

The short-term nature of our earthly existence shouldn't lead us to waste the time we have been given. It should have the opposite effect. It should lead us to make the most of it. Our time is after all a limited commodity. Knowing we have a limited amount of time means that each moment we spend on earthly pursuits is wasted. Likewise, each one we spend on things of spiritual significance is an investment in eternity. Fighting the old man is one of those eternal investments. It is not fruitless. It produces fruit that remains (John 15:16).

There is an old hymn that states "This world is not my home… I am just a' passing through." It is true. We are sojourners. We are aliens here. We must train our minds to think as such. It helps keep all things in perspective. Love our earthly home as we may, there is a *better country* awaiting us. When I get there, my old man will finally be killed. Until that day, the longing for the better country grows stronger, death seems less and less like the enemy, the battle with our old man continues, and we will enjoy more and more personal victories as we grow and mature in our faith.

That isn't so bad, is it?

No. Not at all.

Looking Even Deeper

Personal/Group Discussion and Application

1. Read Revelation 21:1–7.

2. In John's description of a new heaven and earth in Revelation 21, what do you find the most comforting? Why?

3. Why do you think it is so hard for us to remember that we are only temporary residents of this world?

4. How does the promise of heaven help us in our fight against our old man nature?

5. Do you agree with the author that our fight with our old nature is not a "make or break" fight? How so?

6. Pray that God will give you a longing for the better country.

14

Catching the Whistle

To fall in love with God is the greatest romance; to seek him the greatest adventure; to find him, the greatest human achievement.
—Saint Augustine

And amazement seized them all, and they glorified God and were filled with awe, saying, "We have seen extraordinary things today."
—Luke 5:26 (ESV)

The longer I live, the more amazed I become of just how much God loves me. It probably shouldn't be so, at least according to my human reasoning. Ideally, the older I get, the more accustomed to the idea of God's unconditional love I should be growing. You would think that the more instances I accumulate in my lifetime of his forgiveness and restoration would only serve to remind me of this part of his nature. However, every time I fail, every time I look at myself in that mirror of self-disappointment, the more I see just how prone I am to falling and the more utterly astonished I am that God still loves me and wants to do something in my life. I can never get used to it. Instead of getting used to it, the more dumbfounded I am growing. However, along with this puzzlement of mind, the more beautiful his mercy and grace is becoming to me.

I sometimes don't want to live a life in which I am constantly surprised by his mercy. I feel my faith should be stronger. I should expect him to keep his word and be true to his nature and self. At the same time, however, I don't want to ever lose that amazement. I think this is what Jesus had in mind when he told us we are to come to him as little children if we want to come at all (Luke 18:17). Children have a quality that we would all do well to learn and follow. It is the quality of wonder.

One of my favorite pictures is one of my grandson Tristan when he is just a few months old. I am holding him upright in front of my face. All you can see of me is the back of my big head. His face is the focus of the picture. He is staring intently into my face with his eyes wide opened with a look of complete and total amazement and wonder the likes of which only a child of that age can muster. With his eyes opened as wide as they can be and his little mouth cracked open as if about to say something profound, his little hand is reaching for my mouth as if he is about to grab something of great worth. He was trying to capture my whistle.

I was playing with him and making this little bird whistle sound with my lips that I am notorious for making. The sound of that chirping caught his attention, and he was mesmerized. He wanted to touch it. He wanted to hold it. He wanted to know more about it. Even at that young age, his curiosity and wonder were shining through. He wanted to know that whistle. He wanted to experience it. He wanted to feel it. He wanted to grab the whistle. He wanted to capture it and never let it go.

This is that quality that Jesus saw in all children that he wanted us to keep as adults. To be awestruck by God should lead us to only want to know more of him, to reach out and grab that whistle if you will. To keep that attitude of wonder means we never get tired of him or his word and that in time, instead of growing weary of him, we will only want more of him. After all, we have all eternity to get to know him.

Of course, there is a difference between being childlike and being childish. Jesus wasn't asking us to be childish. Childish is being selfish and self-centered. Childish is taking our toys and going home when we don't get our way or having a temper tantrum when we are denied our wants. Childlike, on the other hand, is holding on to the best of childhood, that wonder and amazement that we should have when we look to God.

Childlike means being surprised by the fact that God often answers our prayers in ways we could not predict. It means never losing that wonder at the fact that God forgave me, yet again and that in spite of my failures, he still has a plan for my life. May we all be childlike in our approach to God, especially concerning his forgiveness and in his willingness to use us despite our failures and shortcomings.

In a recent daily reading of the of the Old Testament, I am once again shocked by just how imperfect so many of the great heroes of the faith really were. I mean, let's be honest, some of them were real scoundrels. I have read these stories repeatedly now for close to fifty years and, I still get new insight each time in to just how rotten some of them really were. Like our look at Paul and his thorn, it gives me hope.

For example, Father Abraham basically gave his wife away, saying that she was his sister just to protect himself and his belongings. By the way, his son Isaac which was born of that same woman he tried to give away, would one day do the same thing with his wife. This cowardice is not exactly what you would expect from the two founding fathers of Judaism. Yet God, in his wisdom, chose to include that little side drama in his permanent account of scripture for us to know and from which to learn. He also chose to use both of these men to found the nation of Israel, the Jewish faith and ultimately the Christian faith.

Likewise, Jacob and all his twelve tribal leader sons had family and personal issues, the likes of which would probably disqualify most of them in Christian service if they lived today. Moses, deliverer and lawgiver, was at first a murderer. Years later, King David too was a murderer and adulterer. I'm not even going to discuss his son Solomon. It was a different time I know. But when you read of some of their indiscretions, their drunkenness, their temperament, their relationships, their concubines, and the like, you have to ask the question "What was God thinking when he chose to use them the way he did?" Yet there they are…the patriarchs, the fathers…great heroes of the faith. Through them we would get the great wisdom literature of the Bible and through their lineage would one day come the birth of the Savior of the world, Jesus Christ. Imagine that...

Does this irony take away from the impact of their lives and testimonies and from the reliability of scripture itself? By no means. In fact, it makes it relatable. It makes it real. And it shows God's mercy and patience and love to be even more genuine. If anything, it validates the inspiration of scripture. There is no way man cold come up with these kinds of tragic stories and then effectively sell the lead characters as heroes of the faith. Only God can do that. And he still does it today. This ability God has in seeing past our mistakes and using us to carry out his purposes is part of his nature that sets him and his ways apart from those of mankind.

Like I have probably just done with the above mention of Abraham and the others, we are quick to judge and quick to relegate one's usefulness based on their triumphs and their failures. That is human nature. God's nature is just the opposite. We are told this in one of my favorite passages of scripture, given to Isaiah during a time of exile for the nation of Israel. Isaiah 55:8–9 reads: "For my thoughts are not your thoughts, neither are your ways my ways, declares the LORD. For as the heavens are higher than the earth, so are my ways higher than your ways and my thoughts than your thoughts."

Put simply, God doesn't see things as we do, and we would do well to remember it. His perspective is from a higher advantage than ours.

What this means for us on a personal level is that even when we feel unworthy of God's forgiveness or attention, and we may very well be unworthy and often, we cannot escape the truth that God still gives it. If you have breath in your lungs, then God still has a purpose for you. He still wants to be part of your life and to know you better. Your mistakes don't disqualify you from being important to God and being used of God. You can still have an impact in the kingdom of God.

In fact, scripture teaches us that he is just as awestruck by you as you are of him, if not more so. There are many Bible verses which speak of this. Zephaniah 3:17 speaks of God "rejoicing over you with gladness" and "exulting over you with loud singing." In Psalm 18:19, God rescues us "because he delights" in us. You are the "apple of his eye" in Psalm 17:8. There are many such examples of God celebrating you. Yes, singing over you, shouting over you, dancing over you and delighting over you! And remember, he does this as an all-knowing, all-powerful, holy, and righteous God who knows your words before they reach your tongue; he knows every hair of your head and he knows your past and future failures. In other words, he knows all about you. He has been standing right beside you in those man-in-the-mirror moments when you disappoint yourself and feel as if you have gone too far and there is no going back. He knows all there is to know about you and even more importantly, he still loves you. In fact, I think it is safe to say that he loves you more and more each day.

I know. It's hard to believe. It's sometimes hard to accept. But it is the story of grace. It is God's love story and you are the main character. That old man nature that keeps showing up and causing you problems is not who you are and God knows it. It is not the subject of God's love. You are. It is the new creature you are when you come to Jesus that brings God such joy. The old man is dead. Jesus says, "Behold, I make all things new" (Rev. 21:5). Don't lose the wonder of that reality!

I have to believe that Abraham looked up at that middle eastern night sky, long before the pollution of electric lights and glow from the modern cities would dim the crispness of the night, and he heard God say that his descendants would be as numerous as the stars in the sky or grains of sand on the shore and he thought, "Yeah, right!" How can God do that with me? After all, Abram not yet Abraham, knew his own shortcomings better than anyone else alive. I am sure he had his own man-in-the-mirror moments and his own old man nature to fight. We know he did. Yet God knew him even better that he knew himself. And God has a different view than did Abram or you or me.

I also have to believe, though, that Abram must have looked up at that night sky and all those stars, thinking about the promises of God, and been filled with wonder. Not just at the majestic beauty of the night sky, but at the fact that in all of its vastness and limitlessness, God would take the time to look upon a little man with loads of faults and see him as worthy of his time and attention.

We have an advantage over Abraham. Abraham was still looking forward to his salvation. We, on the other hand, have two thousand years of salvation history to look back upon. The difference for us is that we can see that not only does God see us as worthy of his attention, but he sees us as worth the sacrifice of giving up the glories of heaven for a short hard life on this earth that would ultimately culminate into a death on the cross. He sees us as worth dying for. If we fail to find wonder in that fact, then we fail to understand the gospel!

Don't let the disappointment in yourself rob you of the inestimable joy that should accompany your salvation. Instead, let it reinforce it. Let it remind you of just how much God has done for you and just how much he loves you!

Don't let the old man rob you of the wonder of God's love for you! Be surprised. Be amazed. Be awestruck by God's love for you. Be fascinated. Be overwhelmed. Be dumbfounded. Be astounded. Look into his eyes of grace with eyes wide opened by the wonder of it all. Reach for the whistle!

It is not disrespectful to be shocked by God's love for you. In fact, I would say it is the greatest form of worship we can express. It comes from the heart and is genuine. It is an honor and tribute to our heavenly Father and his Son Jesus Christ. It is praise in its purest form.

So whatever you do, don't let that old nature steal from you the feelings of awe and wonderment and godly fear that comes with your salvation. Fight the old nature. One way to do it is by embracing the wonder. Hold on to it. Don't let go of it. Approach each new day as an opportunity for God to do it again. Look at each sunrise as a new chance that God might surprise you with his love, mercy, and grace today. Open that Bible each time expecting to learn something new, something you have never heard or even thought about before. Expect to hear his voice. Listen for it. Embrace the wonder of walking in newness of life. Embrace the new creation you are in Christ. Be the new creation that God sees when he looks at you. By doing that, you are one step closer to putting that old nature to rest once and for all.

It's time.

It's past time.

Today is the day.

It's time to put it aside.

It is time to live as if your old man is dead. Because he is.

The old man is dead. You are a new creation.

Live the life that God sees when he looks at you.

Looking Even Deeper

Personal/Group Discussion and Application

1. Read Luke 18:15–17.

2. What do you think Jesus meant when he said that we must receive the kingdom of God like a child?

3. How might disappointment in ourselves cause us to lose the wonder and awe of knowing God personally?

4. Do you find yourself amazed by God's love for you? Or do you find yourself having trouble accepting it?

5. Who are some of your favorite biblical heroes? What were their faults?

6. How well do you think you are doing in your struggle against the old man?

7. Pray that God will continue to draw you closer to himself and help you to embrace your identity in Christ.

QUOTE INDEX

(IN ORDER OF APPEARANCE)

"Searcher of Hearts, It is a good day to me when thou givest me a glimpse of myself" (a Puritan prayer taken from *The Valley of Vision*).
Bennett, Arthur ed. 1975. *The Valley of Vision*. Edinburgh, UK: The Banner of Truth Trust, 22.

Chapter 1

"I have never met a man who has given me as much trouble as myself" (Dwight L. Moody).
Moody, Dwight L. 2022. AZQuotes.com. Wind and Fly LTD. May 26, 2022. https://www.azquotes.com/quote/605048.

Chapter 2

"Never trust a dog to watch your food" (St. Patrick).
Saint Patrick. 2022. AZQuotes.com. Wind and Fly LTD. May 26, 2022. https://www.azquotes.com/quote/785655.

I have a word for you. I know your whole
life story. I know every skeleton in your closet.
I know every moment of sin, shame, dishonesty
and degraded love that has darkened your past.

Right now I know your shallow faith, your feeble prayer life, your inconsistent discipleship. And my word is this: I dare you to trust that I love you just as you are, and not as you should be. Because you're never going to be as you should be. (Brennan Manning)

Manning, Brennan. 2005. *The Ragamuffin Gospel* (exclusive 3rd ed.). Sisters, OR: Multnomah Publishers Inc.

"I have light enough to see my darkness, sensibility enough to feel the hardness of my heart, spirituality enough to mourn my want of a heavenly mind; but I might have had more, I ought to have had more."
Bennett, Arthur ed. 1975. *The Valley of Vision* (11th ed.). Edinburgh, UK: The Banner of Truth Trust, 145.

"I sin-Grant that I may never cease grieving because of it."
Bennett, Arthur ed. 1975. *The Valley of Vision* (11th ed.) Edinburgh, UK: The Banner of Truth Trust, 146.

Chapter 3

"Quia amasti me, fecisti me amabilem. (In loving me, you made me lovable.)" (St. Augustine)
Manning, Brennan. 2009. *The Furious Longing of God.* David C Cook, 77.

"Preach the gospel to yourself everyday" (Jerry Bridges).
Bridges, Jerry. 2014. *Holiness Day by Day: Transformational Thoughts for Your Spiritual Journey.* Tyndale House, 41.

Chapter 4

Jesus did not identify the person with his sin, but rather saw in this sin something alien, something that really did not belong to him, something that merely chained and mastered him and from which he would free him and bring him back to his real self. Jesus was able to love men because he loved them right through the layer of mud. (Helmut Thielicke)

Thielicke, Helmut. 2022. AZQuotes.com. Wind and Fly LTD. May 26, 2022. https://www.azquotes.com/quote/736633.

"Habitation of Dragons" (John Owens)
Owen, John. 1842. *The Mortification of Sin in Believers: Containing the Necessity, Nature and Means of It; with a Resolution of Sundry Cases of Conscience Thereto Belonging.*

Chapter 5

"Satan, like a fisher, baits his hook according to the appetites of the fish" (Thomas Adams).
Adams, Thomas, James Sherman. 1848. *An Exposition Upon the Second Epistle General of St. Peter.* 236.

"If God were not my friend, Satan would not so much be my enemy" (Thomas Brooks).
Brooks, Thomas, Jay Patrick Green Sr. 2000. *A Mute Christian Under the Rod & Apples of Gold.* Sovereign Grace Publishers, 87.

"I definitely think that since I've become born again, if you understand in the supernatural realm the spiritual warfare that goes on everyday, I've had far greater challenges on a personal level than before I became a Christian" (Stephen Baldwin).
Funaro, Vincent. 2013. Stephen Baldwin on "I'm in Love with A Church Girl," Ja Rule and Christianity in Hollywood (CP Exclusive). *The Christian Post*, retrieved from christianpost.com.

Chapter 6

"The Christian does not think God will love us because we are good, but that God will make us good because He loves us" (C. S. Lewis).
Lewis, C. S. 2012. *The Complete C. S. Lewis Signature Classics.* HarperCollins, UK, 64.

Chapter 7

"Repentance is the vomit of the soul" (Thomas Brooks).
Thomas Brooks. 1735. *Precious Remedies Against Satan's Devices: Or, Salve for Believers and Unbelievers Sores.* 44.

"The difference between true and false repentance lies in this: the man who truly repents cries out against his heart; but the other, as Eve, against the serpent, or something else" (John Bunyan).
Bunyan, John. 2022. AZQuotes.com. Wind and Fly LTD. May 26, 2022. https://www.azquotes.com/quote/703770.

"All the longer your delay, the more your sin gets strength and rooting. If you cannot bend a twig, how will you be able to bend it when it is a tree?" (Richard Baxter).
Baxter, Richard, William Orme. 1830. *The Practical Works of Richard Baxter: with a Life of the Author and a Critical Examination of His Writings by William Orme.* 11.

"I need to repent of my repentance: I need my tears to be washed" (*Valley of Vision*).
Bennett, Arthur ed. 1975. *The Valley of Vision* (11th ed.). Edinburgh, UK: The Banner of Truth Trust, 136.

Chapter 8

"You should not believe your conscience and your feelings more than the Word which the Lord who receives sinner preaches to you" (Martin Luther).

Luther, Martin. 2022. AZQuotes.com. Wind and Fly LTD. May 26, 2022. https://www.azquotes.com/quote/180806.

Chapter 9

"No matter how dear you are to God, if pride is harboured in your spirit, He will whip it out of you. They that go up in their own estimation must come down again by His discipline" (Charles Spurgeon).

Spurgeon, Charles Haddon. 1988. *Spurgeon at His Best: Over 2200 Striking Quotations from the World's Most Exhaustive and Widely-read Sermon Series*. Baker Publishing Group

> Batter my heart, three-person'd God, for you
> As yet but knock, breathe, shine, and seek to
> mend;
> That I may rise and stand, o'erthrow me, and
> bend
> Your force to break, blow, burn, and make me
> new.
> I, like an usurp'd town to another due,
> Labor to admit you, but oh, to no end;
> Reason, your viceroy in me, me should defend,
> But is captiv'd, and proves weak or untrue.
> Yet dearly I love you, and would be lov'd fain,
> But am betroth'd unto your enemy;
> Divorce me, untie or break that knot again,
> Take me to you, imprison me, for I,
> Except you enthrall me, never shall be free,
> Nor ever chaste, except you ravish me.
> (John Donne)

Donne, John, and C. A. Patrides. *The Complete English Poems of John Donne*. London: Dent, 1985.

Chapter 10

"The perfect church service would be one we were almost unaware of. Our attention would have been on God" (C. S. Lewis).

Lewis, C. S. 2002. *Letters to Malcolm: Chiefly on Prayer*. Houghton Mifflin Harcourt: 8.

Chapter 11

"Jesus promised his disciples three things—that they would be completely fearless, absurdly happy, and in constant trouble" (William Barclay).

Barclay, William. 2022. *The Gospel of Luke Quotes. Quoteslyfe. com*. May 27, 2022. https://www.quoteslyfe.com/quote/Jesus-promised-his-disciples-three-things-that-61616.

Chapter 12

"Do you mortify; do you make it your daily work; be always at it whilst you live; cease not a day from this work; be killing sin or it will be killing you" (John Owen).

Owen, John. 1842. *The Mortification of Sin in Believers: Containing the Necessity, Nature and Means of It; with a Resolution of Sundry Cases of Conscience Thereto Belonging*. 9.

"Ever present now" (Andrew Murray).

Murray, Andrew. 1894. *The Holiest of All: An Exposition of the Epistle to the Hebrews*. New York, NY. Anson d. F. Randolph & Co.

Chapter 13

"If I find in myself a desire which no experience in this world can satisfy, the most probable explanation is that I was made for another world" (C. S. Lewis).
Lewis, C. S. 2022. AZQuotes.com. Wind and Fly LTD. May 27, 2022. https://www.azquotes.com/quote/868180.

> PIPPIN: I didn't think it would end this way.
> GANDALF: End? No, the journey doesn't end here. Death is just another path, one that we all must take. The grey rain-curtain of this world rolls back, and all turns to silver glass, and then you see it.
> PIPPIN: What? Gandalf? See what?
> GANDALF: White shores, and beyond, a far green country under a swift sunrise.
> PIPPIN: Well, that isn't so bad.
> GANDALF: No. No, it isn't.
> (J. R. R. Tolkien)

Tolkien, J. R. R. *The Lord of the Rings: The Return of the King*. www.imdb.com. 2003.

Chapter 14

"To fall in love with God is the greatest romance; to seek him the greatest adventure; to find him, the greatest human achievement" (St. Augustine).
St. Augustine. 2022. AZQuotes.com. Wind and Fly LTD. May 27, 2022. https://www.azquotes.com/quote/363375.

BIBLE CITATIONS

Bible quotes are taken from these noted translations and are marked accordingly:

The Christian Standard Bible. Copyright © 2017 by Holman Bible Publishers. Used by permission. Christian Standard Bible®, and CSB® are federally registered trademarks of Holman Bible Publishers, all rights reserved.

"Scripture quotations are from the ESV® Bible (The Holy Bible, English Standard Version®), copyright © 2001 by Crossway, a publishing ministry of Good News Publishers. Used by permission. All rights reserved. The ESV text may not be quoted in any publication made available to the public by a Creative Commons license. The ESV may not be translated into any other language."

Scripture quotations marked HCSB are taken from the Holman Christian Standard Bible®, Copyright © 1999, 2000, 2002, 2003, 2009 by Holman Bible Publishers. Used by permission. Holman Christian Standard Bible®, Holman CSB®, and HCSB® are federally registered trademarks of Holman Bible Publishers.

The Holy Bible: King James Version. Carol Stream, IL: Barbour Publishing, Inc., 2003.

"Scripture quotations taken from the (NASB®) New American Standard Bible®, Copyright © 1960, 1971, 1977, 1995, 2020 by The Lockman Foundation. Used by permission. All rights reserved. www.lockman.org"

THE HOLY BIBLE, NEW INTERNATIONAL VERSION®, NIV® Copyright © 1973, 1978, 1984, 2011 by Biblica, Inc.™ Used by permission. All rights reserved worldwide.

ABOUT THE AUTHOR

Dr. Rodney Peavy is a native of the state of Georgia. He and his family currently reside in Flowery Branch, Georgia, where he serves as pastor of Macedonia Community Baptist Church. He has served on staff in church ministry since the age of eighteen in varying capacities, including youth ministry, and in both associate and senior pastor positions in churches across the central and north Georgia area. For these many years, his passion has been to fulfill God's vocational call in his life.

Reverend Peavy's educational background includes a master's degree in theological studies from Liberty Baptist Theological Seminary, a bachelor's degree in Christian education, an associate's degree of divinity from the Baptist College of Florida (formerly called Florida Baptist Theological College), and an associate's degree from Truett McConnell College. Also, among his educational achievements, his most personal and most treasured recognition came in the form of an honorary doctor of divinity degree from Grace Bible Institute in his hometown of Buford, Georgia, in 2011.

It was in Graceville, Florida, while attending Florida Baptist Theological College, that Rodney met the woman who would become his wife: Beverly Messer. Rodney and Beverly were married on August 2, 1997. She is a special-education schoolteacher currently serving at Connections Academy in Duluth, Georgia.

The Peavys have four adopted children, three of which are grown and out of the house. They are Christian, Carlos, Tosha, and Joshua. They also have several grandkids.

Prior to this, Rev. Peavy also wrote a book called *Filling the Quiver: Is Adoption God's Will for My Family?* This book is also available through Covenant Books or other usual major retail book avenues and Amazon.

To learn more about the author and his family and ministry, or to sample other writings, please go to www.gospelfoot.com.